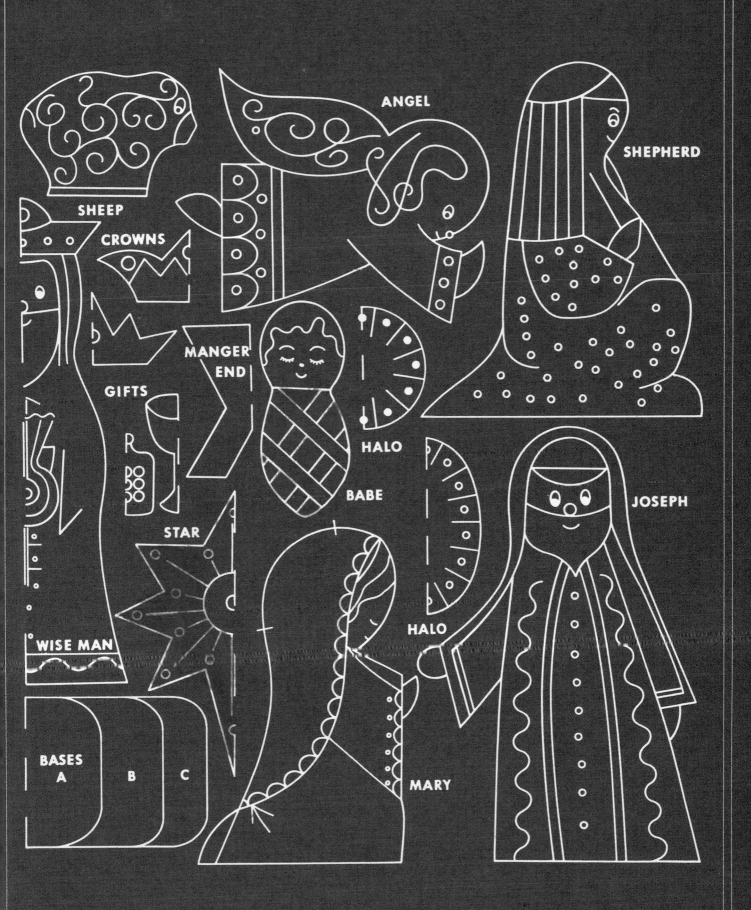

SHEEP

CROWNS

ANGEL

SHEPHERD

GIFTS

MANGER END

HALO

BABE

STAR

HALO

JOSEPH

WISE MAN

BASES A B C

MARY

CHRISTMAS CRAFTS
from McCall's Needlework and Crafts

CHRISTMAS CRAFTS

from
McCall's
Needlework & Crafts

SEDGEWOOD™ PRESS
NEW YORK

For Sedgewood™ Press
Editorial Director, Sedgewood™ Press: *Jane Ross*
Project Directors: *Marilyn Pelo*
Cynthia Vartan
Managing Editor: *Gale Kremer*
Designer: *H. Roberts*
Production Manager: *Bill Rose*

Distributed by Meredith Corporation.

ISBN 0-696-02309-1

Library of Congress Catalog Number 83-51233

Manufactured in the United States of America

10 9 8 7 6 5

CONTENTS

INTRODUCTION

CHRISTMAS is America's favorite holiday. We plan for it, save for it, and anticipate this blessed day weeks in advance. And, as if anyone could forget the date is approaching, stores are all decked out with lavish trim-the-tree boutiques and a mind-boggling display of Christmas merchandise before the Thanksgiving bird has disappeared. This annual commercialism sends the minds of many on a sentimental journey to times that were simpler, more gentle, to those days before Christmas trees came in boxes, before snow and the scent of balsam came in cans. Our alternative: Rekindle the spirit of the holiday tradition by handcrafting your own personalized decorations, the sort that make the holiday truly your own.

The Christmas decoration ideas in this book were chosen for their fresh and imaginative interpretation of favorite, traditional holiday symbols: Santa, reindeer, angels, wreaths, stars, balls, elves, snowmen, the crèche and Nativity figures. These projects cover a wide spectrum of handicraft techniques so that you can choose those that coincide with your interests and abilities.

Because the tree is the focal point of the festivities and decorating it such a family tradition, we start our Christmas crafts with Trimming the Tree, a dazzling array of tree ornaments, so appealing you'll hate to pack them away when the holiday is over.

Next is Decking the Halls, a collection of unexpected suggestions for dressing up your house with eye-catching holiday accessories—from a wreath for the door to a crèche for the mantle and a centerpiece for the table.

Finally, the Filling the Stockings section offers ideas for gifts and stocking stuffers that are fun, easy, and inexpensive to make. The crocheted dolls and animals alone are so irresistible that your only problem will be deciding which of them to make.

Tradition is the foundation of the Christmas season. It is our hope that *Christmas Crafts* will provide many ways for you to start new traditions and to enrich those you already cherish.

TRIMMING THE TREE

Here are tree trimmings you'll hate to put away when the holidays are over. Crochet lacy slipcovers to give plain Christmas balls a new look. Make "gingerbread" cutouts trimmed with rickrack that look good enough to eat. Create dainty beaded snowflakes of white and gold or sparkling feathery snow crystals. Turn embroidered linen and ribbons into ornaments that will be treasured keepsakes. Stored carefully, these and the other dazzling decorations that follow will last for many Christmases.

Tiny Trims

The most inexperienced craftsperson can make little felt cutouts that look like gingerbread and create little people from wooden ice cream spoons.

"Cookie" Ornaments

SIZE: 2¼"-3"

EQUIPMENT: Colored pencil. Pencil. Ruler. Paper for patterns. Small sharp scissors. Toothpicks. Phillips-head screwdriver and hammer (to split wooden beads). Typewriter carbon paper.

MATERIALS (to make ten ornaments as shown): Thin cardboard, 7" × 9" piece. Felt, two 9" × 12" sheets of gold and scraps of green, red, white, and dark brown. White baby rickrack, one 5-yard package. White six-strand embroidery floss, one skein. Scrap of white dotted green fabric. Two tiny lace flower cutouts. Silver-tone small beads, about 65. Red painted wooden beads, ⅜" diameter, six. White glue.

DIRECTIONS: Using sharp colored pencil, draw lines across patterns, connecting grid lines. Enlarge main outlines on paper ruled in 1" squares (see Enlarging the Pattern, page 103); include inner lines, omit zigzag lines, solid dots, flowerettes, and open circles. Center enlarged patterns over cardboard with carbon between; go over main outlines to transfer shapes. Cut out shapes from cardboard and use to cut two gold felt pieces for each main outline. Glue one felt shape to each side of matching cardboard shape; let dry.

Cut embroidery floss into ten 8" lengths; set aside. Working with one ornament at a time, spread glue along cardboard edge and gently press rickrack onto edge, starting at one side; work to bottom, then up and around to starting point; as you approach top, lay center of cut length of floss across edge, to be covered with rickrack. Cut rickrack to butt ends; let dry. Tie floss ends together for

hanger. Cover trumpet handle cutout as for outer edge.

Refer to color photograph and original patterns to decorate one side (or face) of each ornament: Zigzag lines indicate rickrack, solid dots are silver beads, flowerettes at bell top and ginger-girl's head are lace, open circles are red bead halves, other lines indicate felt shapes and felt or fabric strips.

Split wooden beads as follows: Hold point of phillips-head screwdriver in hole at one end of bead, balancing bead on opposite hole. Firmly tap end of screwdriver with hammer, until bead splits in half.

Cut bird wing, stocking cuff, house windows and drumsticks from white felt. Cut five holly leaves, house door and tree trunks, stocking toe and pinwheel pieces from green felt. Cut

tree base, house shutters and two mouths for ginger people from red felt. Cut four eyes for ginger people from brown felt. Cut strips of fabric and felt ⅛″ wide; cut fabric strip for ginger-girl's skirt ½″ wide.

Glue decorations in place, using glue sparingly. Use toothpick as glue applicator for tiny areas and small beads. For horizontal strips, cut felt, fabric, or rickrack a little longer than indicated; glue in place, then trim flush with ornament sides.

Wooden Spoon Ornaments

SIZE: 3¾″ to 6″ tall.

EQUIPMENT: Pencil. Ruler. Tracing paper. Scissors. Dressmaker's tracing (carbon) paper. Dry ball-point pen. Compass. Fine paintbrush. Embroidery and sewing needles.

MATERIALS: Six wooden ice cream spoons. Scraps of cotton fabric in prints and solid white. Felt scraps: red, green, gold, yellow, tan, black, and white. Scraps of white fake fur with long and short piles. White pipe cleaners. Small amounts of white trims: baby rickrack; lace; chenille strand. Small white pompon. Round and oblong pearls. Red and silver seed beads. White glue. Set of acrylic paints. Two white unlined index cards. Sewing thread. Embroidery floss: red, white, and green. One cotton ball. Small twigs.

GENERAL DIRECTIONS: Trace patterns. Complete half patterns where indicated by dash lines. Use dressmaker's carbon and dry ball-point pen to transfer patterns to designated fabrics.

To Make Bodies: Paint face on large end of spoon as shown, using pattern for Carol Singer as a general guide; substitute desired mouth and other features as needed; paint hair as shown for Carol Singer and Angel. For arms, cut a 3″ piece of white pipe cleaner and glue center to center back of spoon. For legs, cut a second piece 4″ long and bend into an inverted "V"; glue point of "V" to middle of small end on all but Baby Jesus; bend ends ½″ for feet. Using pattern, cut four shoe pieces from felt and glue two together at each foot,

sandwiching pipe cleaner between; do not make shoes for Gnome. Finish each figure following individual directions; use coat/dress pattern for garments, except for Baby Jesus; follow solid lines for all except Santa. Make a hanger for each ornament as follows: Thread an embroidery needle with 8″ piece of six-strand floss. Take a small stitch in the headpiece, remove needle, and knot ends of floss together.

CAROL SINGER: Make body, following General Directions. Using pattern, cut four mittens from felt and glue to hands in same manner as for shoes. Cut two dress pieces from print fabric, adding ¼″ all around. Turn edges ¼″ to wrong side and press. With wrong sides facing and folded edges even, glue pieces together, sandwiching body between. Glue chenille trim to skirt and cuffs as shown. Cut a 1⅛″ × ⅞″ piece from index card and decorate for a songbook as shown. Fold book in half and glue to hands. For scarf, cut 6″ × ¾″ strip of green felt and clip into ends to make fringe; glue around neck. For earmuffs, cut two ½″-diameter circles from short-pile fake fur and glue to sides of head. Glue a 1½″ piece of white pipe cleaner around top edge as shown.

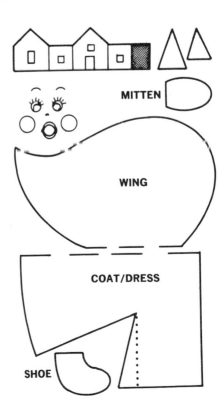

MITTEN

WING

COAT/DRESS

SHOE

ANGEL: Make body, following General Directions. Make dress as for Carol Singer. Trim with rickrack and lace. From index card, cut a circle 1¼″ in diameter; cut, then glue same-size circle of yellow felt to each side to make halo. Glue halo to back of head. Using pattern, cut one double wing piece from card and two from white felt. Glue felt pieces to each side of cardboard wings and trim edges with rickrack as shown. Glue wings to back of Angel. Cut motif from lace and glue to forehead. Trim dress and halo with "pearls" as shown.

MRS. SANTA: Make body, following General Directions. Cut small amount of "hair" from piece of long-pile fake fur and glue around face and on back of head. Cut two dress pieces from red felt; glue together, sandwiching body between; let dry. Trim dress with lace, pearls, and rickrack as shown. Cut a circle 1⅜″ in diameter from felt; baste ³⁄₁₆″ from edge all around. Pull thread to gather into shape of cap; tie off. Glue cap to head. Transfer house and trees to index card and draw a 1″ × ¾″ strip for tray and a ½″ × ¾″ strip for roof. Paint to resemble gingerbread house; cut out. With painted side out, fold house along fine vertical lines and glue shaded tab under adjoining side. Fold roof in half widthwise to make peak and glue, painted side up, on top of walls; let dry. Glue house and trees to tray, propping trees until dry. Decorate roof peak and treetops with red seed beads. Glue tray in hands.

SANTA: Make body, following General Directions. Cut two coat pieces from red felt, following dotted line for narrow sleeves. Glue the two pieces together, sandwiching body between. Cut 1¼″-diameter circle from long-pile fake fur and glue to front of head for beard, completely covering face; brush pile downward. Cut same-size circle of short-pile fake fur and glue to back of head for hair. From red felt, cut 2¼″-diameter circle. Cut circle in half and glue one piece around head,

curved edge down and overlapping ends in back, to make hat. Trim coat and hat as shown, using ¼″-wide strips of white felt. Glue small pompon to point of hat. Cut tiny circle from red felt and glue to face for nose. From green felt, cut small holly leaf and glue to hat, adding small silver bead. For belt, tie white embroidery floss around waist.

BABY JESUS: Paint face, following General Directions. Using the point of a pin, pick a small amount of fuzz from a piece of gold felt and glue to head for hair. Pull apart a cotton ball and glue pieces along lower portion of spoon to pad body. For swaddling, cut fabric circle 3½″ in diameter. Fold an edge of circle ½″ to wrong side and place folded edge at neck, on front of body; wrap piece loosely around body to back and glue edges in place. For sleeves, cut 1″ × 3″ strip from fabric, fold in half lengthwise, trim ends as shown and glue around arms. Glue arms to body, following General Directions. For halo, cut 1¾″-diameter circle from index card. Glue same-size circle of white fabric to each side and glue halo to back of head. Trim halo as shown, using ⅛″-wide strips of yellow felt and "pearls." Cut motif from white lace; glue at neck. Wrap white embroidery floss around body, criss-crossing in front as shown.

GNOME: Make body, following General Directions. Cut two coat pieces from felt; cut away ¼″ from hem edges. From a second color, cut two 1″ felt squares. For each trouser leg, cover one side of a square with glue and fold around leg with raw edges even. Glue the two coat pieces together, sandwiching body between. Glue on red bead "nose" and hair and beard cut from short-pile fake fur. Cover back of head completely with fake fur "hair." Cut felt triangle 2½″ high with 1½″ base. Cover one side with glue and fold around top of head to make hat as shown. For belt, cut red embroidery floss and tie around waist. Tie a small bundle of 1½″ twigs at center and glue in hands as shown.

Snow Crystals

Crochet designs of cotton, then starch them, and trim with beads to make delicate, feathery snowflakes.

Snow Crystals

SIZE: 3″ to 3½″.

MATERIALS: White mercerized knitting and crochet cotton. Steel crochet hook No. 8 (1.25 mm). Silver seed beads or small sequins (optional). Starch or sugar water. All-purpose glue.

STARBURST: Ch 9, sl st in first ch to form ring.

Rnd 1: Ch 5, dc in ring, (ch 2, dc in ring) 6 times, ch 2, sl st in 3rd ch of ch 5—8 sps.

Rnd 2: Ch 1, sc in same st with sl st, * (ch 8, sl st in 4th ch from hook for picot) 3 times, sl st in same ch as first picot, ch 4, sc in same st with last sc, sc in next sp, (ch 10, sc in same sp) twice, sc in next dc, repeat from * around, end sl st in first sc.

DIAMOND: Ch 6, sl st in first ch to form ring.

Rnd 1: Ch 1, 8 sc in ring. Join with sl st in first sc.

Rnd 2: Ch 1, sc in first sc, ch 7, sc in same sc, (sc in next sc, ch 7, sc in same sc) 7 times, sl st in first sc.

Rnd 3: Sl st to 3rd ch of ch 7, ch 1, 2 sc in lp, ch 1, 2 sc in next lp, ch 7, * 2 sc in next lp, ch 1, 2 sc in next lp, ch 7, repeat from * around, end sl st in first sc.

Rnd 4: Ch 1, sc in each of first 2 sc, sc in ch-1 sp, sc in each of next 2 sc, * ch 4, 4 tr in ch-7 lp, ch 4, sc in next 2 sc, sc in ch-1 sp, sc in next 2 sc, repeat from * around, end ch 4, sl st in first sc.

Rnd 5: Ch 1, * sc in each of first 3 sc, (ch 5, sl st in 4th ch from hook for picot) twice, ch 4, sl st in 4th ch from hook, sl st in same ch as last picot, sl st in next ch, make ch-4 picot, sl st in same ch with first picot, sl st in next ch, sc in same sc with last sc, sc in each of next 2 sc, 4 sc in ch-4 lp, ch 4; holding back last lp of each tr, sk first tr, tr in each of next 3 tr, yo hook and through 4 lps on hook (tr cluster made), ch 4, 4 sc in next ch-4 lp, repeat from * around, end sl st in first sc. End off.

CHRISTMAS STAR: Ch 7, sl st in first ch to form ring.

Rnd 1: (Sc in ring, ch 2, dc in ring, ch 2) 6 times. Sl st in first sc.

Rnd 2: Sl st in first 2 ch, sl st in dc, ch 3, dc in same dc, (ch 3, sc in next sc, ch 3, 2 dc in next dc) 5 times, ch 3, sc in next sc, ch 3, sl st in top of first ch 3.

Rnd 3: Ch 3 (counts as 1 dc), dc in next dc, (ch 4, sc in next sc, ch 4, dc in each of 2 dc) 5 times, ch 4, sc in next sc, ch 4, sl st in top of ch 3.

Rnd 4: Ch 3, dc in next dc, (ch 5, sc in next sc, ch 5, dc in each of 2 dc) 5 times, ch 5, sc in next sc, ch 5, sl st in top of ch 3.

Rnd 5: Ch 3, dc in next dc, (ch 7, sc in next sc, ch 7, dc in each of 2 dc) 5 times, ch 7, sc in next sc, ch 7, sl st in top of ch 3.

Rnd 6: Ch 3, dc in next dc, (ch 9, sc in next sc, ch 9; holding back last lp of each dc, dc in each of the next 2 dc, yo hook and through 3 lps on hook) 5 times, ch 9, sc in next sc, ch 9, sl st in first dc. End off.

CLOVER LEAF: Ch 7, sl st in first ch to form ring.

Rnd 1: (Sc in ring, ch 2, dc in ring, ch 2) 6 times, sl st in first sc.

Rnd 2: Ch 1, sc in sc, * ch 3, 2 dc in next dc, ch 3, sc in next sc, repeat from * around, sl st in first sc.

Rnd 3: Ch 1, sc in sc, * ch 4, dc in each of 2 dc, ch 4, sc in next sc, repeat from * around, sl st in first sc.

Rnd 4: Ch 1, sc in sc, * ch 7, dc in each of 2 dc, ch 7, sc in sc, repeat from * around, sl st in first sc.

Rnd 5: Ch 1, sc in sc, * ch 11, dc in next dc, ch 4, sl st in 4th ch from hook for picot, dc in next dc, ch 11, sc in next sc, repeat from * around, sl st in first sc. End off.

CHARMER: Ch 10, sl st in first ch to form ring.

Rnd 1: (Sc in ring, ch 5) 6 times, sl st in first sc.

Rnd 2: Sc in first lp, * (ch 4, sc in same lp) 3 times, sc in next lp, repeat from * around, sl st in first sc.

Rnd 3: Sl st to center of middle lp of first 3 lps; ch 4, 2 tr, ch 4, 3 tr in same lp, * ch 4, 3 tr, ch 4, 3 tr in middle lp of next 3 lps, repeat from * around, ch 4, sl st in top of first ch 4.

Rnd 4: Sl st in next 2 tr; * (sc, ch 4, sc, ch 5, sc, ch 4, sc) in next lp, ch 5, (sc, ch 4, sc) in next lp, ch 5, repeat from * around, sl st in first sc. End off.

SNOW PETALS: Work as for Starburst through rnd 1.

Rnd 2: Ch 1, sc in same st with sl st, * ch 8, sl st in 4th ch from hook for picot, ch 15, sl st in 4th ch from hook for picot, sl st in same ch with first picot, ch 4, sc in same st with last sc, sc in next sp, ch 15, sc in same sp, sc in next dc, repeat from * around, end sl st in first sc. End off.

TWIN STAR: Ch 8, sl st in first ch to form ring.

Rnd 1: (Ch 9, sc in ring) 6 times.

Rnd 2: Sl st in each ch to center of first ch 9, (ch 9, sl st in center of next ch-9 lp) 5 times, ch 9, sl st in first ch of first ch 9.

Rnd 3: Sl st in each of next 2 ch, * ch 14, sl st in 6th ch of same ch-9 lp, ch 9, sl st in 4th ch from hook for picot, (ch 4, sl st in 4th ch from hook) twice, sl st in same ch with first picot, ch 5, sl st in 3rd ch of next ch-9 lp, repeat from * around. End off.

CHRISTMAS DAISY: Ch 9, sl st in first ch to form ring.

Rnd 1: Ch 5, dc in ring, (ch 2, dc in ring) 6 times, ch 2, sl st in 3rd ch of ch 5—8 sps.

Rnd 2: Ch 24, sc in same ch with sl st, * sc in next sp, ch 12, sl st in 4th ch from hook for picot, ch 8, sc in same sp with last sc, sc in next dc, ch 24, sc in same dc, repeat from * around, end sl st in first ch of ch 24 at beg of rnd. End off.

ROSE WINDOW: Ch 10, sl st in first ch to form ring.

Rnd 1: Ch 6, dc in ring, (ch 3, dc in ring) 6 times, ch 3, sl st in 3rd ch of ch 6—8 sps.

Rnd 2: Sl st in next sp, ch 2, 2 hdc in same sp, (ch 2, 3 hdc in next sp) 7 times, ch 3, sl st in top of ch 2.

Rnd 3: Ch 1, turn; sc in first sp, ch 7, sc in same sp, (ch 8, sc in next sp, ch 7, sc in same sp) 7 times, ch 8, sl st in first sc.

Rnd 4: Sl st to 3rd ch of first lp; hdc in lp, (ch 3, sc in 3rd ch from hook for picot, hdc in same lp) twice, * ch 2, sc in next lp, ch 2, hdc, picot, hdc, picot, hdc in next lp, repeat from * around, end ch 2, sl st in first hdc.

Rnd 5: Ch 1, turn; sc in first sp, * ch 4, sc in next sp, ch 5, dc in hdc between 2 picots, ch-3 picot, ch 5, sc in next sp, repeat from * around, end ch 5, sl st in first sc. End off.

FROST CRYSTAL: Ch 12, sl st in first ch to form ring.

Rnd 1: Ch 1, * sc in ring, (ch 5, sl st in 4th ch from hook for picot) 4 times, ch-4 picot, sl st in same ch with last picot, sl st in next ch, (ch-4 picot, sl st in same ch with next picot, sl st in next ch) 3 times, sc in ring, ch 24, repeat from * 5 times, end sl st in first sc. End off.

CHRISTMAS ROSE: Ch 8, sl st in first ch to form ring.

Rnd 1: Ch 7, dc in ring, (ch 5, dc in ring) 4 times, ch 5, sl st in 2nd ch of ch 7—6 sps.

Rnd 2: Sl st in next lp, ch 4 (counts as 1 tr); holding back last lp of each tr on hook, make 3 tr in ch-5 lp, yo and through 4 lps on hook (4 tr cluster), * ch 9, 4 tr cluster in next lp, repeat from * 4 times, ch 9, sl st in top of first cluster.

Rnd 3: * Ch 7, sl st in 4th ch from hook for picot, ch 9, sl st in 4th ch from hook for picot, ch 3, sl st in top of cluster; in ch-9 lp work sc, hdc, 4 dc, hdc, sc, sl st in top of next cluster, repeat from * around, end sl st in sl st at beg of rnd. End off.

BUTTERFLY: Ch 8, sl st in first ch to form ring.

Rnd 1: Ch 4, (dc in ring, ch 1) 7 times, sl st in 3rd ch of ch 4.

Rnd 2: Ch 1, sc in same place as sl st, ch 9, sc in 4th ch from hook for picot, ch 13, sc in sc of picot, ch 4, sc in 4th ch from hook for picot, sl st in ch with previous picot, ch 5, sc in same place as first sc, * (sc in next sp, ch 19, sc in same sp) twice, sc in next dc, ch 9, sc in 4th ch from hook for picot, ch 13, sc in sc of picot, ch 4, sc in 4th ch from hook for picot, sl st in ch with previous picot, ch 5, sc in same dc of ring, repeat from * around, sl st in first sc. End off.

SERENADE: Ch 15, sl st in first ch to form ring.

Rnd 1: Ch 1, 24 sc in ring. Sl st in first sc.

Rnd 2: Ch 1, sc in first sc, (ch 5, sk 2 sc, sc in next sc) 7 times, ch 5, sl st in first sc.

Rnd 3: Sl st in next 2 ch, sc in lp, (ch 5, sc in same lp, ch 5, sc in next lp) 8 times, end sl st in first sc.

Rnd 4: Ch 1, turn; sl st in lp; ch 3, 2 dc, ch 3, 3 dc in same lp, sc in next lp, * (3 dc, ch 3, 3 dc) in next lp, sc in next lp, repeat from * around, end sc in last lp, sl st in top of ch 3.

Rnd 5: Ch 1, turn; sc in sc, * ch 3, 3 dc, ch 3, 3 dc in next ch-3 lp, ch 3, sc in next sc, repeat from * around, sl st in first sc. End off.

GEORGIANA: Ch 7, sl st in first ch to form ring.

Rnd 1: Ch 6, (dc in ring, ch 3) 7 times, sl st in 3rd ch of ch 6—8 sps.

Rnd 2: Sl st in next sp; ch 3, 2 dc in sp, (ch 3, 3 dc in next sp) 7 times, ch 3, sl st in top of first ch 3.

Rnd 3: Ch 7, sk 1 dc, dc in next dc, * ch 4, dc in next dc, ch 4, sk 1 dc, dc in next dc, repeat from * around, end ch 4, sl st in 3rd ch of ch 7.

Rnd 4: Sl st in first sp, ch 4, 2 tr in same sp, ch 4, sc in 4th ch from hook for picot, sl st in last tr, 2 tr in same sp, ch 3, sc in next sp, * ch 3, 3 tr, picot, 2 tr in next sp, ch 3, sc in next sp, repeat from * around, end ch 3, sl st in top of ch 4. End off.

FINISHING: Starch ornaments, pin into shape; let dry. Glue on beads or sequins.

Embroidered Balls

Plastic foam balls can be transformed into distinctive ornaments with embroidered white linen and satin ribbons.

SIZE: 4″ diameter.

EQUIPMENT: Pencil. Colored pencil. Ruler. Scissors. Paper for patterns. Tracing paper. Dressmaker's tracing (carbon) paper. Dry ball-point pen. Embroidery hoop and needle. Straight pins.

MATERIALS: For Each Ball: Plastic foam ball, 4″ diameter. White linen fabric, 16″ square. Desired color satin ribbon, ¼″ wide, 2 yards. Persian yarn in 8.8-yard skeins: one skein each of Christmas red, bright apple green, rosy pink, light amber, toast, midnight blue, regency blue, pure white, black. White glue.

DIRECTIONS: For Each Ball: Using sharp colored pencil, draw lines across embroidery patterns, connecting grid lines. Enlarge patterns by copying on paper ruled in ½″ squares (see Enlarging the Pattern, page 103); trace each separately. For segment pattern, trace and complete actual-size half pattern; cut out. With pencil, lightly mark six segment outlines on linen (two rows of three across), leaving ½″ between each; do not cut out. Center a design in each segment and transfer, using dressmaker's carbon and dry ball-point pen. Place linen in embroidery hoop. Following stitch key (see Stitch Details, page 105), directions, and photograph for colors, embroider designs, using one strand of yarn in needle throughout, except for the following French knots indicated by large dots which require two strands: angel's hair, tree balls, gingerbread buttons, Santa's beard, cuffs, hat brim, and pompon. For Santa, work boots, mittens, belt, nose, and cheeks in satin stitch. When embroidery is completed, cut out all pieces on marked lines.

To construct ball: Apply thin line of glue along edges of embroidered segment. Place top point of segment at center top of foam ball. Press down edges of segment, stretching fabric taut and smooth; make sure that top and bottom points are directly opposite, and pin them in place until glue dries. Continue gluing segments in place until ball is covered with all six pieces. Let dry; remove pins. For

edging, cut ribbon into three 13½″ lengths. Beginning and ending at center top of ball, glue ribbon over raw edges of fabric, pin ends in place. Cut a 10″ length of ribbon; fold in half and glue ends of loop to center top of ball, for hanging. Cut remaining ribbon into three equal lengths and tie into bows; glue bows to top of ball around ribbon loop.

Beaded Snowflakes

These airy snowflakes are white and golden beads strung on copper wire and shaped into forms of delicate beauty.

SIZE: 3½" to 4¾" diameter.

EQUIPMENT: Pencil. Ruler. Wire cutter. Needlenose pliers.

MATERIALS: Round beads size 11/0, 12 strands per bunch, one bunch each; opaque pearl white, transparent gold. Gold-colored wire 28 gauge, one spool.

DIRECTIONS (for each): **Center:** From wire, cut one 11½" length and five 9½" lengths. Carefully pull one strand of desired color beads from bunch; knot thread at one end of strand. At other end of strand, insert 11½" wire through several beads at a time until 18 beads have been strung on one end of wire; carefully pull out thread. Thread other end of wire through beads again. Referring to Diagram 1, pull wire ends until a small circle is formed, leaving a small space as shown; even ends. Cross wire ends and twist together twice, using pliers; separate ends above twist to form a V (see Diagram 2). Attach a 9½" wire to wire circle after every third bead for six V's as shown: Bend wire in half around circle with ends facing outward; twist twice to secure.

Work beading in rounds of triangles and petals, following directions below. As you work, keep beading close and tight so little wire shows. Referring to color illustration, work snowflakes in one color or two; alternate colors as shown or as desired. When all rounds are completed, end off and make hanging loop as directed below.

Triangles: Following individual directions below, thread designated number of beads onto one wire A (see Diagram 2); thread same number onto adjacent wire B. Draw ends of A and B together above beading; then, working with both wires as one, thread on one matching bead, unless otherwise directed; pull wire ends apart to secure beading. Repeat five times for round of six triangles.

Petals: Following individual directions, thread designated number of beads onto each wire of an A or B pair. Hold pencil between beaded wires, then draw together wire ends, so that a beaded petal is formed; remove pencil, then, working with both wires as one, thread on additional beads and secure as for triangle. Repeat five times for round of six petals.

Ending Off: After securing last round of triangles or petals, bend back a pair of ends, then wrap them tightly around wire between the last and next-to-last beads; clip ends and tuck in smoothly. Repeat four times. For hanger, wrap last pair of wires in same manner; do not clip. Using pencil, form hanging loop close to wire ends; twist and clip.

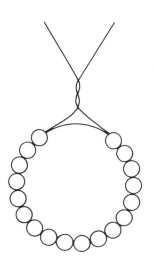

DIAGRAM 1

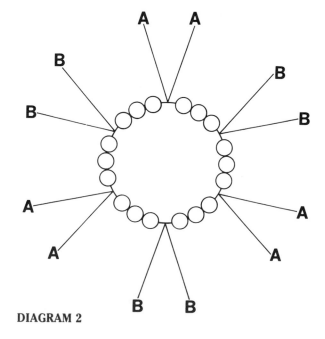

DIAGRAM 2

SMALL WHITE SNOWFLAKE (top left in color photograph): Construct center as directed above.

Round 1: 5-bead triangles.

Round 2: 6-bead triangles.

Round 3: 7-bead petals secured with 6 beads; end off.

LARGE WHITE SNOWFLAKE (bottom center): Construct center.

Round 1: 6-bead petals.

Round 2: 7-bead triangles.

Round 3: 8-bead petals.

Round 4: 8-bead petals secured with 2 beads; end off.

SMALL GOLD SNOWFLAKE (bottom right): Construct center.

Round 1: 5-bead triangles.

Round 2: 6-bead triangles.

Round 3: 9-bead triangles secured with 4 beads; end off.

MEDIUM GOLD SNOWFLAKE (top right): Construct center.

Round 1: 6-bead petals.

Round 2: 8-bead triangles.

Round 3: 8-bead petals secured with 5 beads, end off.

LARGE GOLD SNOWFLAKE (middle left): Construct center.

Round 1: 6-bead triangles.

Round 2: 8-bead petals.

Round 3: 8-bead petals secured with 4 beads; end off.

SMALL GOLD-AND-WHITE SNOWFLAKE (bottom left): Construct center.

Round 1: 7-bead petals.

Round 2: 7-bead triangles.

Round 3: 10-bead triangles.

Round 4: 7-bead petals secured with 3 beads; end off.

LARGE GOLD-AND-WHITE SNOWFLAKE (top center): Construct center.

Round 1: 5-bead triangles.

Round 2: 5-bead triangles.

Round 3: 8-bead petals secured with 3 beads.

Round 4: 8-bead petals secured with 3 beads; end off.

LARGE GOLD-AND-WHITE SNOWFLAKE (middle right): Construct center.

Round 1: 6-bead triangles.

Round 2: 8-bead petals.

Round 3: 8-bead petals secured with 5 contrasting color beads; end off.

Frosted Baubles

Crochet lacy slipcovers—each one as individual as a snowflake—over ordinary tree balls. This is a great way to revive old ornaments that have lost their luster.

SIZE: 2½″ diameter.

MATERIALS: J. & P. Coats Knit-Cro-Sheen, 1 250-yard ball white. Steel crochet hook No. 7. Six Christmas tree balls, 2½″ diameter. Large-eyed needle.

ROSETTE (on blue ball, top right): Beg at center, ch 64. Sl st in first ch to form ring, being careful not to twist ch.

Rnd 1: Ch 1, * sk 3 ch, 8 dc in next ch, sk 3 ch, sc in next ch, repeat from * around, end sk last 3 ch, sl st in each of first 4 dc of rnd—8 shells.

Rnd 2: Sc between 4th and 5th dc, * ch 10, sc between 4th and 5th dc of next shell, repeat from * around, end ch 10, sl st in first sc.

Rnd 3: Sl st in each of next 4 ch, sc in ch-10 lp, * ch 20, sc in next lp, repeat from * around, end ch 20, sl st in first sc.

Rnd 4: Sl st to center of first lp, sc in lp, (sc in next lp) 7 times, sl st in first sc. End off. This end is for bottom of ball.

With lp on hook, sc over first ch of starting ch. Working on opposite side of starting ch, work rnd 1 as for first half, making 8-dc shell in same ch as first half, and working sc over ch and sc between shells. Work rnds 2 and 3 as for first half. End off, leaving 12″ end for sewing.

Run in all yard ends except 12″ end. Run 12″ end through first 10 ch of rnd 3, then through 10th ch of each lp around. Pull cover over ball, pull thread tight around top. Sew end securely.

CENTER BAND (on green ball, top left): Beg at center, ch 72. Sl st in first ch to form ring, being careful not to twist ch.

Rnd 1: Ch 4, sk 1 ch, dc in next ch, * ch 1, sk 1 ch, dc in next ch, repeat from * around, end ch 1, sl st in 3rd ch of ch 4.

Rnd 2: Sl st in next ch-1 sp, ch 4, dc in next sp, * ch 1, dc in next sp, repeat from * around, end ch 1, sl st in 3rd ch of ch 4.

Rnd 3: Repeat rnd 2.

Rnd 4: Sc in next ch-1 sp, * ch 20, sk 5 sps, sc in next sp, repeat from * around, end ch 20, sk last 5 sps, sl st in first sc. End off. Sew center ch of each of 6 ch-20 tog for bottom of ball.

With lp on hook, sc in ch-1 sp on opposite side of band; work as for rnd 4. End off, leaving 12″ end. Run end up through first 10 ch, then through 10th ch of each lp around. Pull cover over ball, pull thread tight around top. Sew end securely.

CRISSCROSS (on red ball, far right): Beg at bottom, ch 6. Sl st in first ch to form ring.

Rnd 1: Ch 4, (dc in ring, ch 1) 13 times, sl st in 3rd ch of ch 4.

Rnd 2: Sl st in first ch-1 sp, ch 3, (dc, ch 2, dc in next ch-1 sp) 13 times, dc in first sp, ch 2, sl st in top of ch 3.

Rnd 3: Sl st in sp between ch 3 and first dc, ch 3, * sk next ch-2 sp, (dc, ch 3, dc in sp between next 2 dc) 13 times, dc in same sp with ch 3, ch 3, sl st in top of ch 3.

Rnd 4: Sl st in sp between ch 3 and first dc, ch 3, * sk next ch-3 sp, (dc, ch 3, dc in sp between next 2 dc) 13 times, dc in same sp with ch 3 at beg of rnd, ch 3, sl st in top of ch 3.

Rnds 5-11: Repeat rnd 4.

Rnd 12: Sl st to center of first ch-3 sp, ch 1, sc in sp, * ch 8, sc in next ch-3 sp, repeat from * around, end ch 8, sl st in first sc. End off, leaving 12″ end. Run end up through first 4 ch, thread through 4th ch of each ch-8 lp around. Pull cover over ball, pull thread tight around top. Sew end securely.

OPEN SHELL (on blue ball, bottom left): Beg at bottom of ball, ch 8. Sl st in first ch to form ring.

Rnd 1: (Sc in ring, ch 10) 8 times, sl st in first sc.

Rnd 2: Sl st to center of first ch-10 lp, ch 3, 2 dc in lp, ch 1, 3 dc in same lp, (3 dc, ch 1, 3 dc in next lp) 7 times, sl st in top of ch 3—8 shells.

Rnd 3: Sl st in each of next 2 dc, sl st in ch-1 sp, ch 3, 2 dc in sp, ch 1, 3 dc in same sp, (3 dc, ch 1, 3 dc in next sp) 7 times, sl st in top of ch 3.

Rnd 4: Repeat rnd 3.

Rnd 5-8: Work as for rnd 3, working shell in shell but ch 1 between shells.

Rnd 9: Repeat rnd 3.

Rnd 10: Sl st to center of shell, sc in ch-1 sp, (ch 8, sc in next ch-1 sp) 7 times, ch 8, sl st in first sc. End off, leaving 12″ end. Run end up through first 4 ch, thread through 4th ch of each ch-8 lp around. Pull cover over ball, pull thread tight around top. Sew end securely.

ZIGZAG (on gold ball, top center): Beg at bottom of ball, ch 8. Sl st in first ch to form ring.

Rnd 1: Ch 4, (dc in ring, ch 1) 7 times, sl st in 3rd ch of ch 4.

Rnd 2: Sl st in first sp, ch 11, (dc in next sp, ch 8) 7 times, sl st in 3rd ch of ch 11.

Rnd 3: * (Ch 1, dc) 6 times in next ch-8 lp, ch 1, sl st in next dc, repeat from * around, end sl st in first ch 1 of rnd—8 scallops.

Rnd 4: Sl st in each st to center ch-1 sp of first scallop, ch 13, (dc in center ch-1 sp of next scallop, ch 10) 7 times, sl st in 3rd ch of ch 13.

Rnd 5: * (Ch 1, dc) 10 times in next ch-10 lp, ch 1, sl st in next dc, repeat from * around, end sl st in first ch 1 of rnd.

Rnd 6: Repeat rnd 4.

Rnd 7: Repeat rnd 3, working in ch-10 lps.

Rnd 8: Sl st in each st to center ch-1 sp of first scallop, sc in center sp, (ch 8, sc in center sp of next scallop) 7 times, ch 8, sl st in first sc. End off, leaving 12″ end. Run end up through first 4 ch, thread through 4th ch of each ch-8 lp around. Pull cover over ball, pull thread tight around top. Sew end securely.

DIAMOND (on gold ball, bottom center): Beg at bottom of ball, ch 8; sl st in first ch to form ring.

Rnd 1: Ch 4, (2 dc in next ch, ch 1) 7 times, dc in last ch, sl st in 3rd ch of ch 4.

Rnd 2: Sl st in first ch-1 sp, ch 1, sc in sp, (ch 7, sc in next ch-1 sp) 7 times, ch 7, sl st in first sc.

Rnd 3: Sl st to center of first lp, sc in lp, (ch 9, sc in next lp) 7 times, ch 9, sl st in first sc.

Rnd 4: Sl st to center of first lp, sc in lp, (ch 11, sc in next lp) 7 times, ch 11, sl st in first sc.

Rnd 5: Work as for rnd 4, making ch 15 lps.

Rnd 6: Repeat rnd 4.

Rnd 7: Repeat rnd 3.

Rnd 8: Sl st to center of first lp, sc in lp, (ch 7, sc in next lp) 7 times, ch 7, sl st in first sc. End off, leaving 12″ end. Run end up through first 4 ch, thread through 4th ch of each ch-7 lp around. Pull cover over ball, pull thread tight around top. Sew end securely.

Pillows of Springtime

Trim the tree with the promise of springtime: Colorful fruits and flowers are worked in easy embroidery stitches, and crisp, white crochet is crowned with flowers of floss. Then both are stuffed like little pillows.

Embroidered Ornaments

SIZE: About 3½" diameter.

EQUIPMENT: Colored pencil. Pencil. Paper for patterns. Scissors. Compass. Dressmaker's tracing (carbon) paper. Dry ball-point pen. Embroidery and sewing needles. Small embroidery hoop. Iron. Padded surface.

MATERIALS (for seven ornaments): White linen fabric 36" wide, ⅝ yard. Small amount six-strand embroidery floss in colors shown in illustration or as desired. Polyester fiberfill. White thread. White satin cord for hanging, 3 yards (15" for each).

DIRECTIONS: Using sharp colored pencil, draw lines across patterns by connecting grid lines. Enlarge patterns by copying on paper ruled in ½" squares (See Enlarging the Pattern, page 103); complete half-patterns indicated by long dash lines. Use compass to make 3"-diameter outlines. For each ornament, mark 4"-diameter circle on right side of linen. Transfer enlarged pattern to center of circle, using dressmaker's carbon and dry ball-point pen; there will be ½" margin all around design outline. Do not cut fabric.

Insert area to be embroidered in embroidery hoop to keep fabric taut. Embroider ornaments, following stitch key in colors shown in photograph or as desired (see Stitch Details, page 105); use two strands of floss in needle. Begin by leaving end of floss on back and working over it to secure. To end strand or begin a new one, weave floss through stitches on back; do not make knots. When embroidery is complete, gently steam-press.

Cut out individual ornaments around 4″ circle. Cut another 4″ circle for backing. With right sides facing, stitch front and backing together ¼″ from edge, leaving opening for turning. Turn to right side, press, stuff lightly, slip-stitch closed. Cut satin cord into 15″ lengths for each ornament; slip-stitch to seam all around, forming a 2″ loop at top for hanging.

Victorian Ornaments

SIZE: 3″ diameter.

MATERIALS: J. & P. Coats Knit-Cro-Sheen, 1 ball white. Steel crochet hooks Nos. 6 and 7. Plastic foam balls, 2½″ diameter. For flowers and leaves, six-strand embroidery floss (colors given with individual directions). Satin and metallic cords. White pearls. Blue beads. Starch. Straight pins.

GAUGE: 10 dc = 1″; 4 rnds = 1″. (To test gauge, see page 108.)

BALL COVER (make 2 pieces): With white and No. 7 hook, ch 4.

Rnd 1: 9 dc in 4th ch from hook. Sl st in top of starting ch.

Rnd 2: Ch 3, dc in same place as sl st, (2 dc in next dc) 9 times. Join with sl st in top of ch 3.

Rnd 3: Ch 3, dc in same place as sl st, (2 dc in next dc) 19 times. Join.

Rnd 4: Ch 3, dc in same place as sl st, dc in next dc, (2 dc in next dc, dc in next dc) 19 times. Join.

Rnd 5: Ch 3, dc in next dc and in each dc around. Join.

Rnd 6: Ch 3, dc in same place as sl st, dc in next 2 dc, (2 dc in next dc, dc in next 2 dc) 19 times. Join.

Rnds 7 and 8: Repeat rnd 5-80 dc.

Rnd 9: Working in front lps, ch 1, * sc in next 2 sc, ch 3, sl st in top of last sc, repeat from * around. Join. Working in back lps of rnd 8, ch 1, sc in each st around. Join; end off. When making 2nd section, leave length of thread for sewing.

Note: Flowers and leaves are made with No. 6 hook.

PURPLE AND PINK BALL:

Violet (make 7): With lavender or purple, ch 5. Sl st in first ch to form ring.

Rnd 1: (Ch 4, 2 tr in ring, ch 4, sl st in ring) 3 times, (ch 5, 2 dtr in ring, ch 5, sl st in ring) twice. End off.

Large Leaf (make 3): With dark green, ch 12. Tr in 4th ch from hook, tr in next 3 ch, dc in next 2 ch, hdc in next ch, sc in next ch, sc, ch 1, sc in last ch. Working along opposite side, sc in next ch, hdc in next ch, dc in next 2 ch, tr in next 4 ch, ch 3, sl st in last ch. End off.

Pink Flower (make 4): Ch 6; join to form ring.

Rnd 1: Ch 1, 12 sc in ring; join.

Rnd 2: Working in back lp, 2 sc in each sc; join.

Rnd 3: Working in back lp, * ch 2, sl st in next sc, repeat from * around. End off. Join thread in any front lp of rnd 1, repeat rnd 3.

Small Leaf (make 3): With light green, ch 9. Sl st in 2nd ch from hook, sc in next ch, hdc in next ch, dc in next 2 ch, hdc in next ch, sc in next ch, sl st in last ch, ch 3. Working along opposite side, sl st in first ch, sc in next ch, hdc in next ch, dc in next 2 ch, hdc in next ch, sc in next ch, sl st in next ch. End off.

BLUE AND WHITE BALL:

Blue Flower (make 8): With light or dark blue, ch 4. Join to form ring.

Rnd 1: * Ch 7; holding back on hook last lp of each tr, 3 tr in 6th ch from hook, yo and

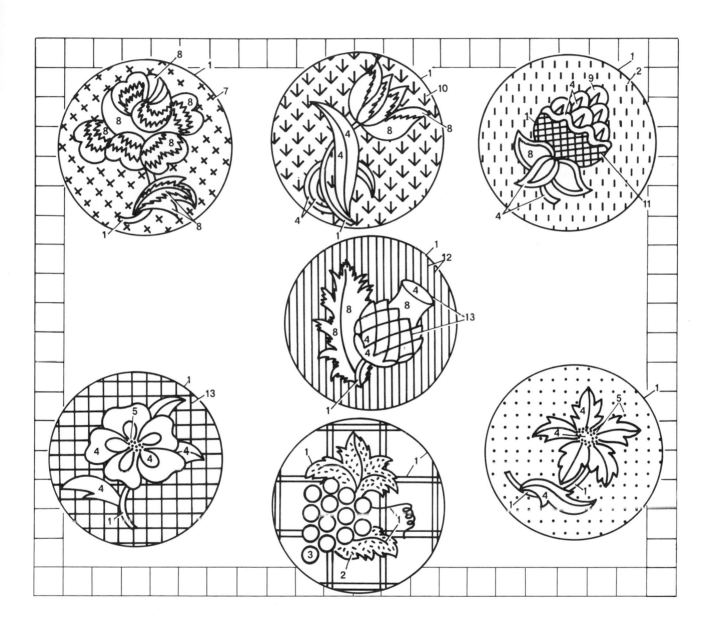

through all loops on hook, sc in ring, repeat from * 4 times—5 petals. End off.

White Flower (make 5): With white, ch 2.

Rnd 1: 8 sc in 2nd ch from hook; sl st in first sc.

Rnd 2: Sc in same place, * ch 2, 2 dc, sc, 2 dc in next sc, ch 2, sc in next sc, repeat from * around—4 petals.

Large Leaf (make 6): With emerald green, ch 10. Sc in 2nd ch from hook, dc in next 7 ch, sc, ch 1, sc in end ch. Working on opposite side of ch, dc in next 7 ch, sc in last ch.

Small Leaf (make 6): With lime green, ch 9. Dc in 4th ch from hook and in next 3 ch, sc in next ch, sc, ch 2, sc in end ch. Working on opposite side of ch, sc in next ch, dc in next 5 ch, sl st in base of ch 3.

CORAL BALL:

Light Coral Flower (make 10): With light coral, ch 5. Dc in 4th ch from hook, ch 3, sl st in same st, sc in next ch (center of flower), (ch 4, dc in 4th ch from hook, ch 3, sl st in same st, sc in same center st) 4 times—5 petals.

Dark Coral Flower (make 6): With dark coral, * ch 4; 2 tr in 4th ch from hook, ch 3, sl st in same ch, repeat from * 9 times—10 petals. End off; leave end for sewing. Thread needle; run thread through base of strip, pull tight to form cluster. Tack tog at base.

Leaf (make 6 each of lime and dark green): Same as small leaf of blue and white ball.

POINSETTIA BALL:

Flower (make 5): With scarlet or dark red, ch 2.

Rnd 1: 8 sc in 2nd ch from hook. Join.

Rnd 2: Ch 7, sc in 2nd ch from hook, hdc in next ch, dc in next 4 ch, sl st in next sc, repeat from * 7 times—8 petals.

Leaf (make 6): With dark green, ch 12. Sc in 2nd ch from hook, hdc in next ch, dc in next ch, tr in next 3 ch, dc in next ch, hdc in next ch, sc in next 2 ch, sc, ch 2, sc in last ch.

Working back in each ch on opposite side, work 2 sc, hdc, dc, 3 tr, dc, hdc, sc.

GOLD BALL:

Flower (make 10): With light, medium or dark gold, ch 5. Join to form ring.

Rnd 1: Ch 1, 12 sc in ring. Sl st in first sc.

Rnd 2: * Ch 3, 5 tr in next sc, drop lp from hook; insert hook in top of ch 3, pull dropped lp through, ch 3, sl st in next sc, repeat from * 5 times—6 petals.

Leaf (make 10): With medium or dark green, ch 10. Sc in 2nd ch from hook, sc in next ch, hdc in next ch, dc in 4 ch, hdc in next ch, sc, ch 3, sc in last ch. Working back in each ch on opposite side, work hdc, 4 dc, hdc, 2 sc.

ROSE BALL:

Irish Rose (make 4): With dark rose, ch 5. Join to form ring.

Rnd 1: Ch 1, 12 sc in ring. Sl st in first sc.

Rnd 2: Ch 1, sc in same place, * hdc, 3 dc, hdc in next sc, sc in next sc, repeat from * 5 times. Join.

Rnd 3: Ch 1, sc in same place, * ch 3, sc in back lp of sc between petals, repeat from * 5 times.

Rnd 4: In each lp make sc, hdc, 5 dc, hdc, sc. End off.

Pink and Rose Flowers (make 9): Work as for light coral flowers.

Leaves (make 8): With dark green, work as for small leaf of blue and white ball.

FINISHING: Wash ball covers, flowers and leaves. Starch using medium starch, 1 part starch, 3 parts water. Cover a plastic foam slab with wax paper. Stretch and mold each ball section over a plastic foam ball, remove carefully to retain shape and set on slab. Stretch and shape all flowers and leaves; pin to slab. Dry thoroughly. Sew ball halves tog over ball (plastic foam or satin ball). Trim with hanging loop and bows of cord attached with pins. Push pins through pearls or beads, then through flower centers. Arrange leaves and flowers as desired and pin to balls.

Bread Dough Trims

You can bake these festive ornaments in your own kitchen from a simple recipe. Mix an extra batch and let the kids invent their own decorations.

EQUIPMENT: Large bowl. Plastic bag. Ruler. Compass. Tracing paper. Small knife. Cookie sheet. Toothpicks. Large and small scalloped cookie cutters. Kitchen grater with small holes (for nest ornament only). Small flat and fine-pointed paintbrushes. Brush for varnish.

MATERIALS: Cookie clay recipe (see below). Fine wire for loops. Tempera or poster paints. Clear gloss varnish.

Cookie Clay Recipe:
4 cups flour
1 cup salt
2 teaspoons mustard powder
1¼ cups water

Using fingers, mix ingredients together in a large bowl. If clay is too stiff, add a little more water. When thoroughly mixed, lift from bowl and knead for five minutes. To prevent drying, put clay in a plastic bag and keep closed until needed.

GENERAL DIRECTIONS: The patterns given here indicate general size and shape. You need not follow them exactly. Pinch off a piece of clay; reclose plastic bag. Roll the clay into a ball in the palm of your hand. Following photograph and drawings, which indicate the separate pieces of each, form the basic shapes. Use small knife and small tools such as manicure equipment. To join pieces, dip fingertip in water; moisten edges of pieces; press together. Follow individual directions for specific details.

Place pieces on cookie sheet for final shaping. When wreaths and ornaments are completed, form short piece of wire into a loop; insert wire ends into top of piece for hanging.

Prick shape with a toothpick in three or four places to prevent uneven rising. Bake at 300°F. for 2 to 3 hours, depending upon thickness of ornament. Test with a toothpick; if still soft, bake a little longer. Let shapes cool completely.

Paint shapes as shown or as desired; leave tan areas in natural cookie color. When paint is completely dry, brush on the varnish or gloss finish as a protective coating. Give ornaments two or more coats, drying between each, depending on amount of glossiness desired.

WREATHS: With compass, draw a ring on tracing paper as indicated in parentheses for individual designs. Make designs of dough and arrange them to fit around traced ring. With water, press them together to secure. Then transfer to cookie sheet.

Santa Heads (8″ diameter, 2″ diameter center): Make entire piece ½″ thick. Add strip for hatband ⅛″ thick, and tiny dot for nose.

Snowmen (7″ diameter, 1½″ diameter center): Make each section ⅝″ thick. Add hatband and three muffler pieces of ⅛″ thickness, and tiny dot for nose.

Trees (9″ diameter, 1½″ diameter center): Make each section ⅝″ thick. Add tiny decorations of ⅛″ thickness.

ORNAMENTS:

Pretzel: From ball, roll a 10″ long, ½″ thick coil of dough. Twist into shape.

Bell: Make each section ½″ thick. Add four pieces for bow ⅛″ thick.

Bird's Nest: With fingers, flatten dough to ¼″ thickness, 2¾″ diameter. For nest, push dough through grater and apply to circle surface. Make bird and eggs ¼″ thick.

Scalloped Wreaths: For each, flatten dough to ¼″-⅜″ thickness. Use cookie cutters to cut out shapes. Add birds of ⅛″ thickness, or sprinkle dough with sesame seeds.

Needlepoint Trims

Stitch up five merry motifs in needlepoint, then pad them for unusual, pillowy decorations.

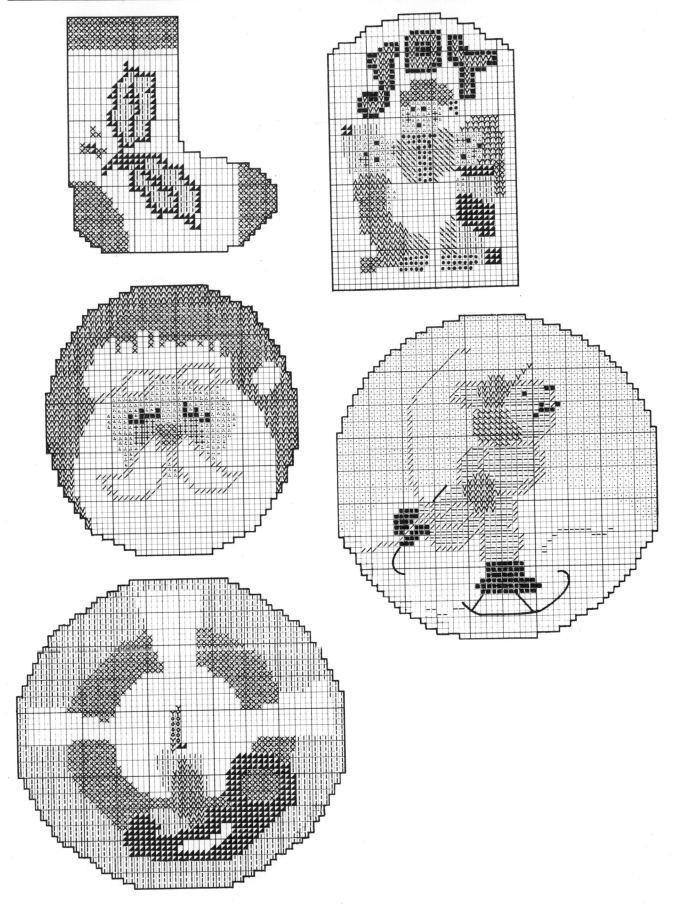

SIZES: Mouse and Candle, 4¼″ diameter; Santa, 4½″ diameter; Stocking, 4¼″ × 3½″; Carolers, 4½″ × 3″.

EQUIPMENT: Ruler. Pencil. Scissors. Masking tape. Tapestry and sewing needles. **For Blocking:** Soft wooden surface. Brown wrapping paper. Rustproof thumbtacks. Square.

MATERIALS: Small amounts of needlepoint canvas: 16-mesh-to-the-inch for Candle and Mouse; 10-mesh-to-the-inch for Santa, Stocking, and Carolers. (**Note:** you can use another mesh canvas if desired; however the mesh will make the ornaments larger or smaller than indicated above.) Persian 3-ply yarn, one 8.8-yard skein or less of each color given in color key, except for 3 of white. Small pieces of felt for each backing (see directions below). Matching sewing thread. Fiberfill or absorbent cotton for stuffing. Narrow satin ribbon for hanging, about 2 yards for all.

DIRECTIONS: Measure, mark, and cut pieces of canvas the size indicated above, adding 2″ all around for margin. Tape edges to prevent raveling. Following color key, charts, and directions below, for working continental stitch, work needlepoint. (Color photograph will be helpful.) Use two strands of yarn for the smaller mesh canvas and three strands for the larger mesh canvas. (**Note:** For Mouse, work needlepoint, then embroider skate blades in backstitch with black, as indicated by solid lines on chart; see Stitch Details, page 105.)

When the needlepoint is finished, block canvas as follows: Cover wooden surface with brown paper. Mark canvas outline on paper for guide, being sure corners are square. Mark horizontal and vertical center lines of marked outline on paper and canvas. Place canvas right side down over guide; match center markings on canvas with those on paper. Fasten canvas with tacks about ½″ to ¾″ apart along edge of canvas, stretching canvas to match guide. If yarn is not colorfast, apply salt generously. Wet thoroughly with cold water; let dry.

To assemble each ornament, trim canvas margin to 1″. Cut piece of felt the same size as canvas piece. With right sides facing, sew edges together with 1″ seam, leaving opening at top for turning and stuffing. Trim seams to ⅜″ and clip at curves. Turn to right side. Stuff fully.

To make hanging loop, cut 6½″ length of ribbon; fold in half and insert ends ¼″ into opening at top. Slip-stitch opening closed, securing ribbon loop at same time. Cut another 6½″ length of ribbon; tie into bow and tack at top of ornament in front of loop.

Continental Stitch: Start at upper right corner and work across to left. Bring needle out to front of canvas at point that will be bottom of first stitch; needle goes under two meshes of canvas, diagonally, as shown. Details show placement and direction of needle; turn work around for return row. Always work from right to left.

Continental Stitch

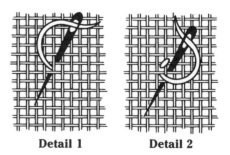

Detail 1   Detail 2

P A R T II
DECKING THE HALLS

Start your own holiday traditions. Tell the joyous Christmas story with a crocheted folk-art crèche. Give the tree a distinctive look with a candlewick skirt and an angel for the top. Or say "Merry Christmas" with an edible crèche shaped from delicious gingerbread. Adorn your table with perky gingham accessories. Hang lots of stockings by the chimney (with care) and create decorations uniquely your own to enjoy year after year.

Folk-Art Crèche

Recreate the Nativity scene with tiny figures crocheted in sparkling jewel colors.

SIZE: 6″-7″ tall.

MATERIALS: DMC Brilliant Crochet Cotton, 1 ball each of yellow #8729, white, flesh pink #8739, red #8741, purple #8742, aqua #8719, olive #8728, tan #8776, brown #8722. Steel crochet hook No. 3. Fiberfill or batting. Squares of felt and cardboard, 3½″ square for each figure. Pipe cleaner for shepherd's staff. Tapestry needle. Sewing needle and threads.

GAUGE: 8 sc = 1″. (To test gauge, see page 108.)

GENERAL DIRECTIONS: When body piece is finished, fold it so ends of rnds are at center back. Sew tog across top of shoulders. Stuff firmly. Cut a circle of cardboard and one of felt (3¼″ diameter for Mary and angel, 2¾″ for king, 2¼″ for Joseph and shepherd). Slip cardboard circle into bottom of figure, top with felt circle; sew felt to last rnd. Sew neck of head to center top of figure. Sew arms to each side of shoulders. Mantles and cloaks will drape better if sizing is removed by rinsing in warm water. Squeeze out excess moisture; dry flat. Shape in folds around figure; hold in place with a few stitches. Starch halos and wings lightly before sewing in place. Embroider eyes with straight sts or sew on small beads.

MARY: HEAD: With flesh pink, ch 2.

Rnd 1: 8 sc in 2nd ch from hook. Do not join rnds.

Rnd 2: 2 sc in each sc around—16 sc.

Rnds 3-6: Sc in each sc around.

Rnd 7: (Sc in next sc, sk next st) 8 times.

Rnd 8: Sc in each sc. End off. Stuff firmly.

BODY: Beg at waist, with red, ch 16. Sl st in first ch to form ring.

Rnd 1: Sc in each ch.

Rnd 2-5: Work even on 16 sc.

Rnd 6: (Sc in 3 sc, 2 sc in next sc) 4 times.

Rnds 7-9: Work even on 20 sc. End off.

Skirt: Join red in first ch of body. **Note:** Ch 3 at beg of each rnd counts as first dc. Join each dc rnd with sl st in top of ch 3.

Rnd 1: (Dc in 3 ch, 2 dc in next ch) 4 times.

Rnd 2: (3 dc, 2 dc in next dc) 5 times—25 dc.

Rnd 3: Dc in each dc around.

Rnd 4: (4 dc, 2 dc in next dc) 5 times—30 dc.

Rnd 5: Repeat rnd 3.

Rnd 6: (5 dc, 2 dc in next dc) 5 times—35 dc.

Rnd 7: Repeat rnd 3.

Rnd 8: (Dc in 3 dc, 2 dc in next dc, dc in next 3 dc) 5 times—40 dc.

Rnd 9: Repeat rnd 3. End off.

Rnd 10: With white, (sc in 4 dc, 2 sc in next dc) 8 times—48 sc. Sl st in first sc. End off.

Rnd 11: With olive, sc in each sc around. Sl st in first sc.

Rnd 12: Ch 1, repeat rnd 11. End off.

Rnd 13: Join red, ch 6, (sk 1 st, 5 dc in next st; drop lp off hook, insert hook in last ch made, pick up dropped lp and draw through, ch 3) 23 times, 4 dc in same st as ch 6, sl st in 3rd ch of ch 6, complete last popcorn with lp from sl st. End off.

Rnd 14: With olive, work 3 sc in each ch-3 sp. Sl st in first sc. End off.

Rnd 15: With white, (4 dc, dec 1 dc in next 2 sc) 12 times—60 dc. End off.

Rnd 16: With olive, sc in each st around. End off.

Rnd 17: With white, repeat rnd 16.

Rnd 18: With olive, repeat rnd 16.

ARMS: (make 2): With red, ch 2.

Rnd 1: 8 sc in 2nd ch from hook. Do not join rnds.

Rnds 2-7: Work even on 8 sc.

Rnd 8: Inc 1 st in rnd.

Rnd 9-11: Work even on 9 sc.

Rnd 12: Inc 1 st in rnd.

Rnd 13: Work even on 10 sc. End off.

Rnds 14 and 15: With white, work even.

Rnd 16: With olive, work even. End off. Join pink in last rnd on opposite side from where color changes were made, ch 3, 4 dc in same st, drop lp from hook, insert hook in top of ch 3, pick up dropped lp and draw through. Ch 1 to fasten. End off.

MANTLE: With aqua, ch 36.

Row 1: Dc in 4th ch from hook (counts as 2 dc), dc in each ch across. Ch 3, turn.

Rows 2-17: Sk first dc, dc in each dc across, dc in top of turning ch. Ch 3, turn each row. At end of row 17, ch 1, do not turn.

Edging: Rnd 1: Sc around, working sc in each st on ends, 3 sc in each corner, and 2 sc in each row. End off.

Rnd 2: With red, sc in each sc around, 3 sc in each corner. End off.

Rnd 3: With aqua, repeat rnd 2.

HAIR: Cut about 40 strands yellow 11″ long. After sewing head to figure, sew center of strands to center of head, beginning at forehead and working back. Braid strands each side; tie ends with red.

HALO: With white, ch 4. Sl st in first ch to form ring.

Rnd 1: Ch 3, 11 dc in ring. Sl st in top of ch 3.

Rnd 2: Ch 5, (dc in next st, ch 2) 11 times, sl st in 3rd ch of ch 5.

Rnd 3: Ch 1, (2 sc, ch 3, sl st in first ch of ch 3, 2 sc in next ch-2 sp) 12 times. End off.
   See General Directions for finishing.

ANGEL: Make head and body as for Mary, substituting white for red, purple for olive and yellow for white. Make halo with yellow.

HAIR: Join brown where hairline should be. (Ch 3, sc in next st) around head, forming hairline. (Ch 4, sc in next st) around head in row behind first row; continue to work around until top of head is covered.

WINGS: (make 2): With yellow, ch 13.

Row 1: Sc in 7th ch from hook, (ch 3, sk 2 ch, sc in next ch) twice. Ch 1, turn.

Row 2: (Tr in center ch-3 sp, ch 1) 7 times. Sl st in last ch-3 sp. Ch 1, turn.

Row 3: 2 sc in same ch-3 sp, (2 sc in next ch-1 sp) 8 times, 2 sc in ch-3 sp. Ch 3, turn.

Row 4: (Sk next sc, sc in next sc, ch 3) 9 times. Do not turn.

Row 5: Working across straight edge, 2 dc in side of sc row, (4 dc in ch-2 sp) 3 times, 2 dc in side of sc row, dc in ch-3 sp on outer edge—18 dc. Ch 3, turn.

Row 6: Dc in dc below ch 3 (inc made), dc in each st across—19 dc. Ch 6, turn.

Row 7: (Sk 2 sts, tr in next st, ch 2) 5 times, tr in last st. Ch 3, turn.

Row 8: Dc, sc, 2 dc in first ch-2 sp, (ch 1, 2 dc, sc, 2 dc in next ch-2 sp) 5 times. Ch 8, turn.

Row 9: (Tr in next ch-1 sp, ch 4) 5 times, tr in last dc. Ch 1, turn.

Row 10: (Sc, dc, 3 tr, dc, sc in ch-4 sp, sl st in tr) 6 times. End off.

Horn: With yellow, ch 15. Join to form ring. Sc in each ch around. Work even on 15 sc for 2 more rnds. Dec 1 st each rnd until 3 sts remain. End off. With red, work 1 rnd sc on opposite side of starting ch. With yellow, work 1 rnd sc, inc 1 st; work 2 more rnds even. End off.

JOSEPH: Make head as for Mary.

BODY: Beg at shoulders, with olive, ch 24. Join to form ring.

Rnd 1: Sc in each ch around.

Rnds 2-5: Work even on 24 sc.

Rnd 6: (Sc in next 5 sts, 2 sc in next st) 4 times. Sl st in first sc of rnd. Ch 3. **Note:** Join all dc rnds with sl st in top of ch 3 (first dc).

Rnds 7-9: Dc in each st around.

Rnd 10: (Dc in 6 sts, 2 dc in next st) 4 times.

Rnds 11-13: Work even on 32 dc.

Rnd 14: (Dc in 7 sts, 2 dc in next st) 4 times.

Rnds 15-17: Work even on 36 dc.

Rnd 18: (Dc in 8 sts, 2 dc in next st) 4 times.

Rnds 19 and 20: Work even on 40 dc. End off.

Rnd 21: With white, (sc in next 9 sts, 2 sc in next st) 4 times—44 sc. End off.

Rnds 22-24: With brown, work even on 44 sc. End off.

ARMS (make 2): With olive, ch 4. Sl st in first ch to form ring.

Rnd 1: Ch 1, 12 sc in ring.

Rnds 2-6: Work even on 12 sc.

Rnd 7: Inc 1 st.

Rnds 8 and 9: Work even on 13 sc.

Rnd 10: Inc 1 st.

Rnds 11 and 12: Work even on 14 sc.

Rnd 13: Inc 1 st.

Rnds 14 and 15: Work even on 15 sc.

Rnd 16: With white, work 1 rnd.

Rnds 17 and 18: With brown, work 2 rnds. End off.

Hands: Join pink in last rnd on opposite side from color changes. Ch 4, 4 tr in same st, drop last lp off hook, insert hook in top of ch 4, pick up dropped lp and draw through. Ch 1 to fasten. End off.

MANTLE: With red, ch 25.

Row 1: Sc in 2nd ch from hook and in each ch across, changing to tan in last sc. With tan, ch 1, turn. Cut red.

Rows 2-24: Sc in each st across, changing from tan to red each row.

Edging: With brown, sc around, working sc, ch 1, sc in each corner. Join; end off.

Rnd 2: Join purple, ch 3, work dc in each st around, making 2 dc, ch 1, 2 dc in each corner sp. Join; end off.

Rnd 3: With red, sc around, making 3 sc in each corner sp. Join; end off.

Beard: See directions for angel's hair. With brown, make 2 rows of ch-3 lps around chin.

SHEPHERD: Make head as for Mary.

BODY: With tan, work as for Joseph through rnd 18.

Rnd 19: With white, work even in sc.

Rnd 20: With red, work even in dc.

Rnd 21: With brown, work even in sc.

Rnd 22: With tan, work in dc, inc 4 dc evenly around.

Rnd 23: Work even in dc. Join; end off.

ARMS: Work as for Joseph, substituting tan for olive, brown for white, red for brown.

MANTLE: With red, ch 26.

Row 1: Dc in 4th ch from hook and in each ch across. Change to olive by drawing lp of olive through last 2 lps on hook. Cut red. With olive, ch 3, turn.

Rows 2-12: Work in dc, alternate 1 row olive with 1 row red. End off.

Edging: Work as for Joseph's mantle, working 2 sc in each dc row on first rnd. Work rnd 1 in brown, rnd 2 in white, rnd 3 in red.

Staff: Cover 6″ pipe cleaner with brown thread, wrapping thread closely around. glue ends to hold thread. Curve top around a pencil.

LAMB: HEAD: With white, ch 2.

Rnd 1: 8 sc in 2nd ch from hook.

Rnd 2: Work even on 8 sc.

Rnd 3: Inc 2 sc in rnd.

Rnd 4: Work even on 10 sc.

Rnd 5: Inc 1 sc in rnd.

Rnd 6: Work even on 11 sc.

Rnd 7: Dec 3 sts evenly spaced.

Rnd 8: Dec 4 sts even spaced. End off. Stuff.

BODY: Ch 4. Join to form ring. Ch 1, 12 sc in ring. Continue to work even on 12 sc until body is 1½". Dec in every 2 sts until tube is enclosed. End off. Stuff.

Ears: * Join white in 7th rnd of head. Ch 3, dc in each of next 2 sts, drop lp off hook, insert hook in 3rd ch of ch 3, draw dropped lp through. Ch 1 to fasten. End off. Sk 1 st on rnd, repeat from *. Sew back of head to 2nd rnd of body.

Legs: With white, ch 15. Sc in 2nd ch from hook and in each ch across. End off. Sew center of strip to 3rd rnd of body on opposite side from head.

KING: Make head with brown or pink as for Mary's.

BODY: With purple, work as for Joseph's body through rnd 8.

Rnd 9: (Dc in 6 sts, 2 dc in next st) 4 times—32 dc.

Rnd 10: Dc in each dc around.

Rnd 11: (Dc in 7 sts, 2 dc in next st) 4 times—36 dc.

Rnd 12: Repeat rnd 10.

Rnd 13: (Dc in 8 sts, 2 dc in nxt st) 4 times—40 dc.

Rnd 14: Repeat rnd 10. End off.

Rnd 15: With yellow, sc in back lp of each st. End off.

Rnd 16: With red, (sc in back lp of 3 sts, dc

in front lp of next st of rnd 14) 10 times. End off.

Rnd 17: With aqua, (sc in back lp of next st, dc in front lp of next st of rnd 15, sc in back lp of next 2 sts) 10 times. End off.

Rnd 18: With purple, (9 dc, 2 dc in next st) 4 times—44 dc. End off.

Rnd 19: With yellow, sc in each st around. End off.

Rnd 20: Join red, ch 6; (sk 1 st, 5 dc popcorn in next st; see rnd 13 of Mary's skirt; ch 3) 21 times, 4 dc in same st as ch 6, sl st in 3rd ch of ch 6, finish popcorn. End off.

Rnd 21: With aqua, 2 sc in each ch-3 sp. End off.

Rnd 22: With purple, (dc in 10 sts, 2 dc in next st) 4 times—48 dc. End off.

Rnd 23: With yellow, sc around. End off.

Rnd 24: With aqua, (11 dc, 2 dc in next st) 4 times—52 dc. End off.

ARMS: (make 2): With purple, work as for Joseph through rnd 8.

Rnd 9: Inc 1 st.

Rnd 10: Work even on 14 sc.

Rnd 11: Inc 1 st.

Rnd 12: Work even on 15 sc.

Rnd 13: Inc 1 st. End off.

Rnd 14: With red, work even on 16 sc.

Rnd 15: Inc 1 st. End off.

Rnd 16: With yellow, work even on 17 sc. End off.

Rnds 17 and 18: With aqua, work even. End off. Work hands as for Joseph.

CLOAK: With olive, ch 12.

Row 1: Dc in 4th ch from hook and in each ch across. Ch 3, turn.

Row 2: Work even in dc.

Row 3: Inc 1 dc each side—12 dc.

Row 4-6: Work even in dc.

Row 7: Repeat row 3—14 dc.

Rows 8 and 9: Repeat row 4. End off.

Row 10: Join yellow, repeat row 3. End off.

Edging: Join red at top corner; sc around 2 long sides and wide end, making 3 sc in each bottom corner. Sew narrow end of cloak across shoulders.

CROWN: With yellow, ch 18. Join to form ring, sc in each ch around. Work even for 2 rnds.

Rnd 4: (Ch 4, sl st in 3rd ch from hook, ch 1, sk 1 sc, sc in next st) 9 times, end sl st in first ch. End off. Sew crown to head.

GIFT: With white, ch 2.

Rnd 1: 8 sc in 2nd ch from hook.

Rnd 2: 2 sc in each sc around—16 sc.

Rnds 3 and 4: Work even. Drop white.

Rnd 5: With red, work even. Drop red.

Rnd 6: With white, work even. Drop white.

Rnd 7: Repeat rnd 5.

Rnd 8: With white, dec 4 sc evenly spaced. End off.

Rnds 9 and 10: Repeat rnd 5. End off.

Cover: With yellow, repeat rnds 1–3. End off. Stuff gift; sew on cover. Sew bead to top.

INFANT: Work head as for Mary.

BLANKET: With white, make as for shepherd's mantle, omitting color change.

Edging: Work as for Joseph's mantle, substituting yellow for brown, aqua for red. Wrap blanket around ball of stuffing about 3 times as large as head. Sew tog, forming body. Sew head to body, concealing neck in fold of blanket. Make halo as for angel and sew to top of head.

PILLOW: TOP: With aqua, ch 4. Join with sl st to form ring. At beg of each rnd, ch 3 for first dc. Sl st in top of ch 3 at end of rnd.

Rnd 1: (4 dc in ring, ch 2) 4 times.

Rnd 2: (Dc in each st across, 2 dc, ch 2, 2 dc in ch-2 sp) 4 times.

Rnd 3: Repeat rnd 2. End off.

Rnd 4: With red, repeat rnd 2.

Rnd 5: With purple, repeat rnd 2.

Rnd 6: With yellow, repeat rnd 2. End off.

BOTTOM: Work as for top, using tan for rnds 1–3, brown for rnd 4, purple for rnd 5, red for rnd 6.

Joining: With purple, sc pieces tog through edges of both pieces, making 3 sc in each corner sp. Stuff pillow lightly before sc rnd is completed. Sew infant to pillow.

Gingerbread Crèche

A charming crèche to bake—and eat—when Christmas is over. The figures are decorated with brightly colored icing.

EQUIPMENT: Tracing paper. Pencil. Ruler. Lightweight cardboard. Scissors. Aluminum foil. Sifter. Large saucepan. Mixing spoon. Three cookie sheets (or use one three times). Rolling pin. Sharp knife. Pastry brush. Tea strainer. Paper toweling. Bowls for icing. Electric beater. Pastry tube with tips for writing and making small circles. Toothpicks.

MATERIALS: Gingerbread Dough and Decorating Icing (see recipes on next page). Tea. Package of flaked coconut. Instant coffee. Vegetable food dyes. Silver dragées.

DIRECTIONS: Trace patterns on next page; complete half-patterns indicated by dash lines. For each wise man, make separate pattern using same body but placing crown and gift in place for each (see photograph). Cut patterns out of cardboard. Make patterns for stable of cardboard as follows: For sides, cut piece 4½″ × 13″; for back, cut a triangle with 5½″ base, 13″ tall; for large shingle, cut piece 1½″ square; for small shingle, cut piece ¾″ × 1⅝″; for top, cut piece ½″ × 4¾″; for loft, cut piece 2½″ × 4¼″. For manger side, cut piece 1¾″ × 1″. Cover patterns with foil.

Gingerbread Dough:

5 cups sifted all-purpose flour
1 teaspoon baking soda
1 teaspoon salt
1 teaspoon nutmeg
3 teaspoons ginger
1 cup shortening
⅔ cup sugar
1 cup molasses

Sift together flour, baking soda, salt, nutmeg, and ginger. Melt shortening in large saucepan over moderate heat (about 250° F.). Add sugar and molasses; stir well. Remove from heat. Gradually stir in 4 cups of flour mixture until thoroughly combined. Work in remaining flour mixture with hands. Chill overnight.

The next day, preheat oven to 375° F. Place ⅓ of dough on ungreased cookie sheet. Roll dough into ¼″ thick rectangle on cookie sheet. Place pattern pieces on rectangle of dough and, using sharp knife, cut around patterns carefully. Cut one of each piece except for the following: cut two sheep; cut two manger ends and two manger sides. Cut two of base A; cut five of base B (cut one of base C). Cut two large side pieces; cut 50 large shingles; cut 20 small shingles. Remove excess dough. You will need three cookie sheets with rectangles of dough rolled out on each to make all these pieces. Place cookie sheets with cutouts in oven and bake 13–15 minutes or until lightly browned. Do not remove pieces from cookie sheets until completely cooled.

Make a sugar glue to hold pieces together as follows. Put sugar in saucepan and melt over low heat. Using pastry brush, brush one edge of back triangle with sugar and very quickly place one side on and hold for a couple of seconds (it hardens very quickly). Dip inner surface of each shingle in melted sugar and, working from bottom up, quickly press onto side of stable to form roof. Alternate large and small shingles as desired and make them overlap each preceding row. Repeat with other side and remaining shingles. Put melted sugar on the two side edges of loft piece and quickly slide it in place. Brush bottom surface of rooftop piece with melted sugar and place on top. With melted sugar, secure manger sides to end pieces, star to stable top.

To make floor for entire creche, cut piece of heavy cardboard 10½″ × 16½″. To simulate straw, make a strong blend of tea: place package of coconut in tea and let steep about 15 minutes; strain; dry on paper toweling. Thin sugar glue with a little water and spread on floor cardboard. Sprinkle floor with coconut-tea mixture; add instant coffee for dirt. Glue coconut-tea mixture on loft and manger bottom.

Decorating Icing:

2½ cups confectioner's sugar
¼ teaspoon cream of tartar
2 egg whites
½ teaspoon vanilla

Sift together sugar and cream of tartar in large bowl. Add egg whites and vanilla. Beat until very stiff. Cover with damp cloth until ready to use.

When ready to decorate, place amounts of icing in individual bowls (one for each color); leave icing in one bowl white and add food dyes, small amounts at at time, to other bowls of icing until desired shades are blended. With knife, carefully spread icing to cover areas such as faces, hands, beards, crowns, star, and Babe's clothing. With icing in tube with writing tip, make lines of design as shown in photograph and as indicated on patterns. Make dots of icing by dabbing icing (with circle tip) where indicated by circles on patterns. For the smallest details, such as the mouths and Babe's facial features, dip toothpick directly into food dye and paint. Work carefully. Secure silver dragées to star center and to wise men's crowns and to one gift as shown with white icing. Add green icing to floor to simulate grass.

When figures have been iced and are dry, dip bottom of figure into melted sugar and press immediately onto base. The largest base is for the kneeling shepherd; the two small bases are for the sheep; the remaining bases are for the remaining figures (except for angel and Babe). Spread melted sugar on top of each base and sprinkle the coconut-tea mixture on it. With melted sugar, secure halo to Mary and to Babe. Place Babe in manger.

Spread melted sugar on back surface of angel and press onto front top of stable: hold until secure.

To make staffs for Joseph and the shepherd, dye piece of thin spaghetti for each in tea; secure in place with melted sugar.

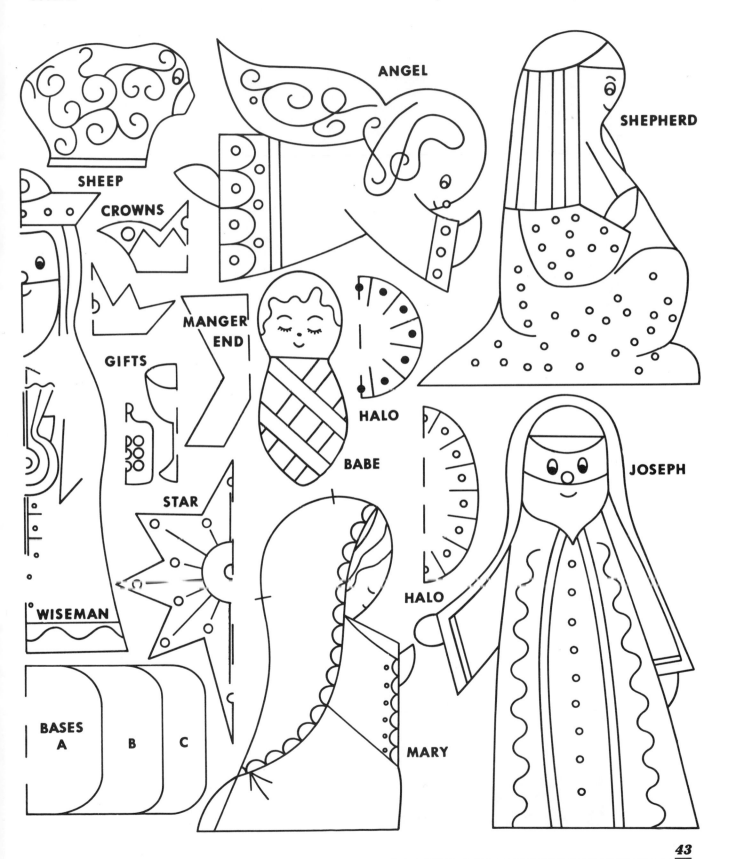

SHEEP

CROWNS

ANGEL

SHEPHERD

GIFTS

MANGER END

HALO

BABE

STAR

HALO

JOSEPH

WISEMAN

BASES A   B   C

MARY

Christmas Candlewick Designs

Dress your tree in candlewicking, a truly American form of embroidery, updated here with color and simple stitchery.

SIZE: Tree skirt, 39½" diameter. Stocking, 21" long. Angel, 12" high.

EQUIPMENT:

For All: Pencil. Ruler and yardstick. Paper for patterns. Tracing paper. Black waterproof marking pen. Water-erasable pen. Plant sprayer with water. Embroidery and regular scissors. Sewing and embroidery needles. Straight pins. Sewing machine. Iron. Small safety pin.

For Skirt: Compass. Thumbtack. String.

For Angel: Knitting needle or small crochet hook.

MATERIALS:

For Each: 4-strand candlewick yarn, one 50-yard card each of crimson and leaf green; one card natural for angel. Ecru sewing thread. Quilt batting. Lightweight unbleached muslin 38" wide, satin ribbon, ecru ruffled eyelet trim.

For Skirt: Muslin, 2¼ yards. Ribbon, 5/16" wide, 4¼ yards crimson. Eyelet, 1½" wide, 3⅓ yards.

For Stocking: Muslin, 1½ yards. Ribbon, ¼" wide, 2 yards cream. Eyelet, 1½" wide, 5/8 yard.

For Angel: Muslin, ¾ yard. Ribbon, ⅛" wide, ⅓ yard cream. Eyelet, 1" wide, ½ yard. Two small black seed beads. Round gold-color threading beads ⅛", about 55. Polyester fiberfill for stuffing.

GENERAL DIRECTIONS: Draw lines across each pattern, connecting grid lines. Enlarge pattern by copying on paper ruled in 1" squares (see Enlarging the Pattern, page 103). Make a tracing of pattern; darken lines with waterproof marker. Cut piece from muslin for front, following individual directions. Center piece over tracing with design lines showing through. Using water-erasable pen, transfer outlines of piece (heavy lines on original paper) and embroidery lines (fine lines and heavy dots). Cut out ¼" beyond outlines for seam allowance. Cut same-size pieces from muslin and batting as directed.

To Embroider: Pin and baste one piece of batting to wrong side of front piece. Work embroidery through both thicknesses, following stitch key (see Stitch Details, page 105) and photograph for colors. Work French knots (heavy dots on patterns) with all four strands of yarn doubled in needle (eight strands); use two strands of yarn for all other embroidery, unless otherwise directed. For stitched ribbon "casing" (ladder-type designs), work top edge in outline stitch, then work blanket stitch to form bottom edge and "rungs."

When all embroidery is complete, dampen front piece with sprayer to erase ink; iron gently to dry. Assemble and finish each piece as directed below. Cut ribbons as directed and use safety pin to work through casings; even ends. Cut eyelet as directed; slip-stitch straight edge to lining so that ruffle extends beyond edge of piece.

TREE SKIRT: Read General Directions. Enlarge quarter-pattern for skirt; using compass or thumbtack and string, mark arcs the following distances from corner X (see pattern): skirt, 18½"; center opening, 4¼"; also mark arcs for design lines: A, 4½"; B, 4⅞"; C, 12"; D, 12⅜"; E, 16¼". Cut 38" square from muslin; fold into quarters, press to crease, then unfold. Transfer tracing to one quarter of muslin, omitting dash lines. Rotate pattern and muslin 90° to mark next quarter; repeat twice more. Cut out skirt front as directed; do not cut slit. Cut muslin lining and batting same size as muslin front. Baste batting to front piece and work embroidery. When all embroidery is complete, erase ink; press.

To Assemble: Baste lining to right side of skirt front. Mark a slit (folding circle into quarters) and cut through all thicknesses. Stitch outer curved edge and slit edges, making ¼" seams. Clip across corners; trim excess batting close to stitching and ¼" from raw inner edges; turn skirt to right side. Press raw edges ¼" to inside; slip-stitch opening closed. Cut eyelet to fit outer edge of skirt, plus ½"; press ends under ⅛" twice; topstitch; sew in place. Cut two pieces of ribbon to fit casings, plus 12" for ties.

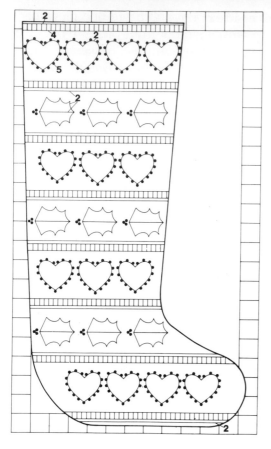

STOCKING: Read General Directions. Prepare stocking pattern. Cut 13″ × 23″ piece from muslin. Transfer pattern for front; cut out as directed. Cut three more stockings from muslin for back and lining and two from batting. Baste batting to front and back pieces; work embroidery on front. When all embroidery is complete, erase ink; press.

To Assemble: Cut eight pieces of ribbon to fit casings, adding ½″ to each length; insert and baste in place through seam allowance. Pin stocking front and back together with muslin pieces facing and edges even; stitch around sides and bottom, making ¼″ seam. Trim excess batting close to stitching and ¼″ from raw top edges; turn to right side. Stitch remaining stockings together for lining; do not turn. Fold and press all raw edges ¼″ to wrong side. Insert lining into stocking with folded edges even; slip-stitch stocking top to lining all around. Cut eyelet to fit around top, plus ½″; sew in place, overlapping ends. Cut two 14″ pieces of ribbon for hanging loop and bow. Form a loop with one ribbon, overlapping 3½″ from ends; tack at overlap to left side of stocking top. Tie second ribbon into bow; tack in place.

STITCH KEY

1 Straight Stitch 5 French Knot
2 Outline Stitch 6 Satin Stitch
3 Fly Stitch 7 Couching
4 Blanket Stitch 8 Open Cretan Stitch

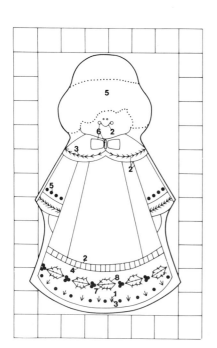

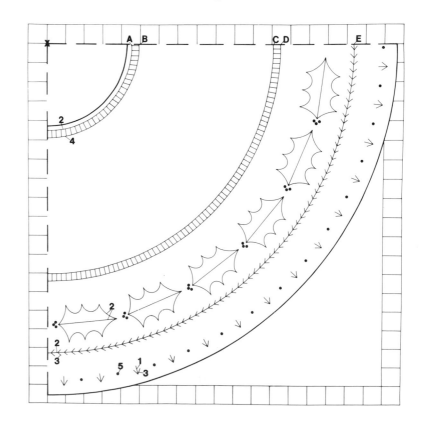

TREETOP ANGEL: Read General Directions. Prepare pattern for angel. Cut 9″ × 13″ piece from muslin. Transfer pattern for front; cut out as directed. Cut three more angels from muslin for back and lining and two from batting. Baste batting to front and back pieces; work embroidery on front, using only one strand in needle for mouth and cheeks. When all embroidery is complete, sew on black beads for eyes; sew on two rows of gold beads for halo (see illustration). Erase ink; press. With scissors, carefully make small slits in batting between rows of stitches in face, upper sleeves, and main portions of gown; do not cut into front piece beneath. Using knitting needle or small crochet hook, poke fiberfill through slits, carefully pushing it into corners and curves of each outlined section. Do not overstuff. Check front of design as you work to make sure stuffing is evenly distributed. After stuffing each section, whipstitch slits closed.

To Assemble: Cut ribbon to fit casing, plus ½″; insert and tack in place through seam allowance. Construct and assemble angel and lining in similar manner as for stocking, except leaving opening in hem edges. Cut eyelet to fit hem, plus ½″; sew in place, overlapping ends. Stuff head with fiberfill until firm.

Quick-Stitch Calico Fun

A festive tea cozy and pot holder, holiday scene pillows, and bow-topped 'package' pillows, all quick to stitch by machine.

EQUIPMENT: Pencil. Colored pencil. Ruler. Paper and cardboard for patterns. Scissors. Dressmaker's tracing (carbon) paper. Dry ballpoint pen. Tracing wheel. Straight pins. Sewing and embroidery needles. Sewing machine with zigzag attachment. Iron.

MATERIALS: Closely woven cotton or cotton-blend printed fabric such as calico, 45" wide: see individual directions for amounts. Fusible webbing. Six-strand embroidery floss, small amounts of yellow, gold, red, green, blue, black, orange. White thread. Batting.

GENERAL DIRECTIONS: Using sharp colored pencil, draw lines across patterns by connecting grid lines. Enlarge patterns by copying on paper ruled in 1" squares (see Enlarging the Pattern, page 103). Heavy solid lines indicate cutting lines; fine lines indicate embroidery (and position of ribbon on tea cozy).

Using dressmaker's carbon and dry ballpoint pen, transfer complete pattern to right side of one piece of background fabric, centering design; do not cut out. Trace each separate part of design; complete pieces where they overlap. Glue tracings to cardboard and cut out for appliqué patterns. Place cardboard patterns on fabric and mark around with pencil; cut out appliqués on pencil lines. Cut piece from fusible web same size as each appliqué. Place appliqués over fusible web on right side of background fabric in marked positions, overlapping as indicated. Following package instructions, fuse appliqués to fabric. Notice how individual pieces overlap; be sure to lay them in proper order. Stitch around appliqués, covering edges with small white zigzag (satin) stitch. Embroider appliqués where indicated. (See Stitch Details, page 105.)

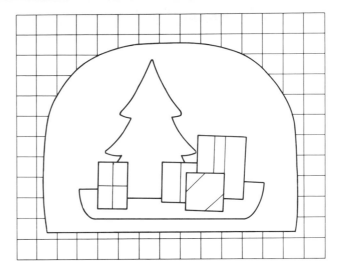

TEA COZY AND POT HOLDER: Blue

calico, 1¼ yards; muslin for interlining, ¾ yard; scraps of green, yellow, blue, and red calico; scrap of solid white fabric. Lace, ¾″ wide, 1 yard. Red ribbon, ½″ wide, ½ yard.

Using dressmaker's carbon and tracing wheel, mark outline only of tea cozy four times on wrong side of blue calico, and twice on fabric for interlining; mark two 6¼″ squares for pot holder on calico and two on interlining. Leave at least ½″ between all pieces. Cut out pieces, adding ¼″ for seam allowance.

For quilting, mark intersecting diagonal lines ¾″ apart on right side of two calico tea cozy pieces and both pot holder squares. Cut batting ¼ smaller than each piece to be quilted. Place each interlining piece on flat surface; center batting over interlining; place calico over batting, right side up. Baste through all three layers around perimeter and diagonally across pieces. Machine-quilt.

Following General Directions, cut, fuse, and stitch appliqués to one quilted tea cozy and one pot holder piece; for tea cozy, cut grosgrain ribbon in half and place an end on each piece underneath an appliqué as indicated; tie bow.

To finish tea cozy, embroider packages as indicated on pattern, using two strands of floss in needle. Embroider two long straight stitches for ribbon; anchor crossing with cross-stitch.

For ruffle, machine-baste close to one long edge of lace; pull bobbin thread to gather lace

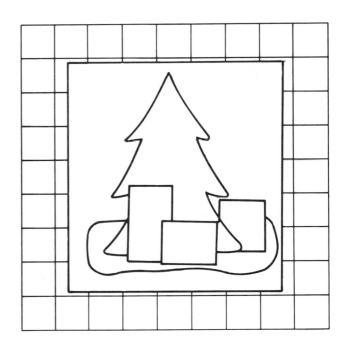

to fit around curved edge of one tea cozy piece. Pin gathered edge of lace to curved edge; stitch together ¼″ from edge. With right sides facing and with lace in between, pin two quilted pieces together, matching raw edges. Stitch around curved edge, making ¼″ seam; clip curves.

For lining, stitch remaining two pieces of calico together in same manner, omitting lace. Turn lining to right side and slip over quilted piece with wrong sides facing. Pin raw edges together, and stitch ¼″ from edges, leaving a 3″ opening. Turn right side out; slip-stitch opening closed. Insert lining inside.

For pot holder, cut 1″ × 3″ strip from green calico for loop. Turn long raw edges ¼″ to wrong side and press; turn again enclosing raw edges, and topstitch down center of strip. Fold strip in half crosswise; with raw edges even, baste ends of loop to right side of front piece at top right corner. Pin the two quilted pieces together with right sides facing and raw edges flush; stitch ¼″ from edges, leaving a 3″ opening on one side. Turn to right side; slip-stitch opening.

FIREPLACE AND TREE PILLOWS: For each: white calico, ¾ yard; red calico, 4″-wide strips sewn together to equal 2½ yards; scraps of green, brown, rust, black, red, yellow, navy, beige, and blue calico.

For Tree Pillow: Yellow rickrack, ¼″ wide, ⅓ yard.

For background of each, mark two pieces on white calico, each 13¼″ × 12¼″; cut, adding ¼″ seam allowance. Appliqué one piece for each, following General Directions. Using two strands of contrasting embroidery floss in needle, embroider packages as indicated on patterns, using satin and straight stitches for ribbons and large bows, lazy daisy stitches for small bows. (See Stitch Details, page 105.)

For fireplace pillow, use orange stem stitch for cat's tail, orange and black straight stitches for whiskers, and one orange fly stitch for each eye.

For tree pillow, glue three strips of yellow rickrack across tree as in photograph, turning raw edges under ⅛″.

To finish each pillow, fold 2½-yard strip in half lengthwise with wrong sides facing and press. Machine-baste edges together ⅛″ and again ¼″ from raw edges. Pull bobbin thread to gather fabric to fit around perimeter of background piece. With raw edges even, pin gathered ruffle to right side of appliquéd background; adjust gathers and stitch ¼″ from raw edges. With right sides facing and ruffle in between, pin two background pieces together, matching raw edges. Stitch ¼″ from raw edges, leaving 3″ opening in one side. Turn right side out and stuff pillow with batting until plump. Turn raw edges of opening ¼″ to wrong side; slip-stitch opening.

PACKAGE PILLOWS: Cut background fabric and contrasting strips according to sizes given in individual directions, adding ¼″ seam allowance. Turn long edges of strips ¼″ to wrong side and press. Pin wrong side of strips to right side of one background piece as directed, with raw edges of strips even with raw edges of background. Stitch strips to background close to folded and raw edges. Pin background with strips to matching background piece, right sides facing and raw edges even. Stitch together ¼″ from raw edges, leaving 3″ opening in one side. Turn right side out; stuff with batting until plump. Turn raw edges of opening ¼″ to inside; slip-stitch opening closed. Turn all edges of remaining strip ¼″ to wrong side and press; turn under again, enclosing raw edges, and topstitch close to folded edges. Tie finished strip into a bow.

Red Pillow: Red calico, ⅝ yard; white calico, two strips 1⅞″ × 11½″; one strip 2⅜″ × 36″. Cut two background pieces from red, each 9¾″ × 15″. Pin finished 11½″ white strips to background diagonally at each corner, as shown in photograph; trim excess fabric so edges of strips are even with edges of background. Finish pillow as directed; slip-stitch bow to center of one strip.

White Pillow: White calico, ¾ yard; dotted navy, one strip 2″ × 13½″, one strip 2″ × 12½″, one strip 2½″ × 44″. Cut two background pieces from white, each 12½″ × 13½″. Center two finished blue strips between each side of background, so strips cross at right angle in center. Finish pillow as directed; slip-stitch bow to top edge of one strip.

Blue Pillow: Blue calico, ⅓ yard; cream calico, one strip 2½″ × 19¾″, one strip 2½″ × 9½″, one strip 3″ × 44″. Cut two background pieces from blue, each 9½″ × 19¾″. Center finished cream strips between each side of background, so strips cross at right angle in center. Finish pillow as directed; slip-stitch bow to top end of one short strip.

Decorative Stockings

Eight stockings sure to catch St. Nick's attention are made four different ways: knit, crochet, Weave-It and punch-needle embroidery on needlepoint canvas.

Punch Needle Stockings

FINISHED SIZES: Panda, 14″ long. Holly, 18″ long. Christmas Themes, 21″ long.

EQUIPMENT: Waterproof marking pen. Masking tape. Scissors. Needlepoint frame (or artist's stretcher frame to fit canvas, plus staple gun and staples). Sewing and tapestry needles. Russian punch needle. Sewing machine.

MATERIALS: Needlepoint interlocking canvas, 12 mesh-to-the-inch, 13″ × 18″ for Panda, 14″ × 20″ for Holly, 18″ × 23″ for Christmas Themes. Fake fur, ½ yard for each, white for Panda and Holly, red for Christmas Themes. Yarns: For Panda: Bucilla's Perlette, scarlet #6, ½ skein; white #1, ¼ skein; also black mohair yarn, about ¼ skein. For Holly: Bucilla's Perlette, white #1, ½ skein; also 3-ply fingering yarn, light and dark green, ¼ skein each. For Christmas Themes: Bucilla's Perlette, spearmint #9 and white #1, ½ skein each; bright yellow #11 and scarlet #6, ¼ skein each; also small amounts of either Persian, crewel, fingering, or baby yarn in following colors: gray, black, pink, dark green, pale yellow, and rust. Small amounts of red and yellow narrow ribbon and white lace. Red ½″-diameter plush balls (as from small ball fringe), 18. Fold-over braid, 1″ wide: 1 yard red for Panda, 1½ yards white for Holly, 1½ yards red for Christmas Themes. Brush-on latex glue. Red and white sewing thread.

GENERAL DIRECTIONS FOR NEEDLEPOINT PUNCH (punch needle on canvas):

To Prepare Canvas: Bind all canvas edges with masking tape. Baste center row of holes vertically and horizontally between canvas threads. Each square on chart represents one hole in canvas; arrows on chart indicate center of canvas, which is sometimes a space, sometimes a thread. Counting spaces on chart from center rows outward and using waterproof pen, transfer stocking outline and inner designs to canvas. Place canvas marked side up in needlepoint frame or staple to artist's stretcher frame, keeping canvas taut and threads straight.

To Use Yarn Needle: Read manufacturer's directions. Practice punching on scrap canvas. Set plastic stitch guide so that ½″ of needle extends for loops and ¾″ of needle extends for flat stitches. Loop stitches are punched from the wrong side of the canvas and create a raised design on the right side; flat stitches are punched from the right side. When punching, guide needle in and out of canvas holes, pushing all the way down until plastic guide hits the canvas; raise needle to the surface and draw or drag needle tip over canvas thread to next hole. Keeping the needle eye always facing away from the next hole to be punched, so that you trail the yarn.

To Work Design: Following individual directions, work all raised or loop sections first from the wrong side of the canvas. Each area is generally outlined and then filled in with Vertical or Horizontal Stitch; see below. Then work flat stitches; if frame can be turned over and you can work comfortably from right side, do so; if not, carefully remove canvas, turn over and re-staple canvas, right side up. Work flat stitches in Diagonal or Vertical Stitch; see below. When work is finished, clip thread close on back; do not make knots. Remove mistakes by pulling out stitches; do not reuse yarn. Take canvas off frame and cut unworked canvas, leaving a 1″ margin all around. Coat wrong side of work with latex glue and let dry.

TO WORK STITCHES:

Outlining Stitch: Work a continuous line, punching in each hole and following the contour of the shape to be filled.

Vertical Stitch: Start from lower right corner of area to be filled. Punch first row from bottom to top, going in each hole; move over one hole to left and punch second row from top to bottom, going in each hole. Continue in this manner until area is filled.

Horizontal Stitch: Work as for Vertical Stitch but in horizontal rows, punching every hole from right to left for one row and left to right for the next.

Diagonal (or "Mosaic") Stitch: Starting from lower right or left, punch a diagonal row to top, going in each hole; move over one hole to the right or left and punch second row to bottom, going in every other hole. Repeat these two rows to fill area. For a **Wide Diagonal Stitch,** work in a four-row pattern, going in each hole for rows one and two and every other hole for rows three and four.

PANDA STOCKING: Read all General Directions. Following General Directions, prepare canvas, transfer design, and mount in frame, marked side up. Referring to chart and color key, work Panda in Vertical Stitch as follows: Work facial features, then outline and fill in face and ears. Work white areas of body, then black areas, outlining each area first. Punch a guideline (any color) one row of spaces around stocking outline. Turn canvas over to work from right side. Punch background inside guideline in Wide Diagonal Stitch. Make small red yarn bow and tack under Panda's chin. Pull out guideline loops. Following General Directions, remove work

from frame, trim canvas edges, and coat with glue.

To Make Stocking: Cut stocking back from fake fur same size as stocking front, so pile side will face out. With wrong sides facing, baste stocking front to back, stitching close to last row of punch work; leave stocking top open. Trim seam allowance to ¼" all around. Pin fold-over braid around stocking edges, encasing raw edge and overlapping seam (leave stocking top open); topstitch through all thicknesses. For cuff, measure inside circumference of stocking opening; cut fake fur piece ½" longer than measurement and 5" wide. With right side inward, sew short ends of cuff together, making a ¼" seam. Turn one long edge ¼" to wrong side and slip-stitch in place for cuff hem. Slip cuff into stocking top, so that right side of cuff faces wrong side of stocking and raw edges are even. Hand or machine stitch cuff and stocking edges together. Pull cuff out and fold over stocking edge.

HOLLY STOCKING: Read all General Directions. Following General Directions, prepare canvas, transfer design, and mount in frame, marked side up. Referring to chart and color key, work leaves in Vertical Stitch: Holly leaves are either light green, outlined and detailed in dark green, or dark green, outlined and detailed in light green. For each leaf, work outlines and details in the contrasting color first, indicated on chart by dots, then fill in with main color. Large squares covering four meshes indicate placement for "berries"; leave these meshes blank. Punch a guideline (any color) one row of spaces around stocking outline. Turn canvas over to work background from right side. Punch background inside guideline in Wide Diagonal Stitch. Tack plush balls in place for "berries." Pull out guideline loops. Following General Directions, remove work from frame, trim canvas edges, and coat with glue. Make stocking as for Panda.

CHRISTMAS THEMES STOCKING: Read all General Directions. Following General Directions, prepare canvas, transfer design, and mount in frame, marked side up. Chart is keyed with numbers for color of large design

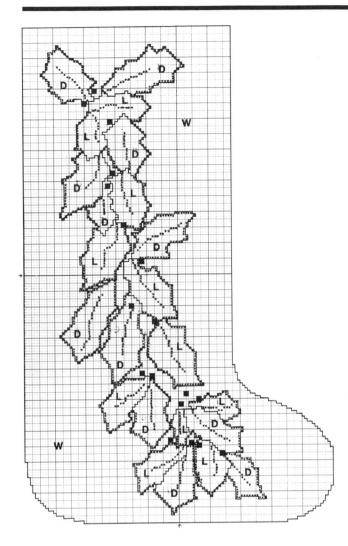

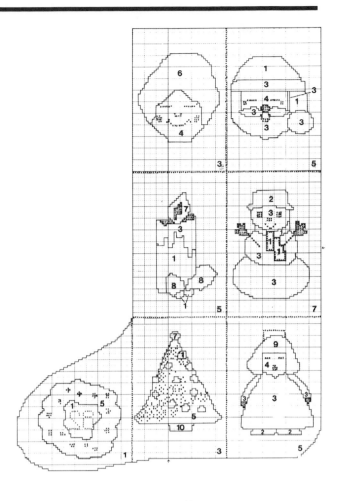

Continental Stitch

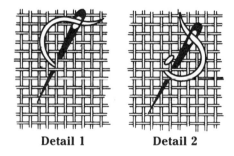

Detail 1   **Detail 2**

areas and backgrounds, and dots for border rows and details. Using Scarlet Perlette in tapcstry needle, work border rows in needlepoint Contintental Stitch (see detail); work vertical rows first, then horizontal rows. Work "84" in wreath with white and halo over angel in gold in same stitch. Following General Directions for needlepoint punch, work details as indicated below, then outline and fill in larger areas of each motif as keyed, using Vertical or Horizontal Stitch as desired; do not fill in background. Work Santa's eyes in black, nose, mouth, and cheeks in scarlet; following key, outline and punch face, beard, and hat. Work Momma's eyes and nose in black, mouth and cheeks in scarlet, then work face and hair. Work Snowman's eyes and mouth with gray, nose in bright yellow; outline scarf in black and work arms and hands in gray; complete, following chart. Work

center of candle flame and top of candle in scarlet; complete. Work angel's eyes in black, mouth in scarlet, hands in pink; complete. Work tree balls in scarlet and dotted areas in dark green; complete. Work wreath balls in scarlet; outline and fill in wreath.

Punch a guideline (any color) one row of spaces around stocking outline. Turn canvas over to right side, following General Directions. Punch backgrounds in Wide Diagonal Stitch with colors indicated. Following illustration, tack small yellow bow and a bit of lace under Momma's chin, a long red bow under angel's chin, and a yellow bow to wreath top. Using yarn in tapestry needle, make red fringe at lower edges of Snowman's scarf. Pull out guideline loops. Following General Directions, remove work from frame, trim canvas edges, glue. Make stocking as for Panda.

Red Knit Stocking

SIZE: 20″ long.

MATERIALS: Knitting worsted, 1 4-ounce skein red. Knitting needles No. 7. Two stitch holders. 1″ ball fringe, ¾ yd. each of blue and gold. Sewing thread.

GAUGE: 5 sts = 1″, 6 rows = 1″. (To test gauge, see page 111.)

STOCKING: Beg at upper edge, cast on 60 sts. Work in ribbing of k 1, p 1 for 6 rows. Work in stockinette st (k 1 row, p 1 row) for 7″, dec 1 st each side on next row, then every 1″ 3 times more—52 sts. Work even until piece is 13″ long, end k row.

Divide for Heel: Left Heel Half: Row 1: P 13 sts. Sl next 26 sts on a holder (instep), sl last 13 sts on another holder for right heel half. Work on left heel half only.

Row 2: Sl 1, k 12. Repeat last 2 rows 8 times.

Next Row: P 2, p 2 tog, p 1, turn; sl 1, k 3, turn; p 3, p 2 tog, p 1, turn; sl 1, k 4, turn; p 4, p 2 tog, p 1, turn; sl 1, k 5, turn; p 5, p 2 tog, p 1, turn; sl 1, k 6, turn; p 6, p 2 tog, p 1—8 sts. Cut yarn; sl sts on a safety pin.

Right Heel Half: Sl sts of right heel to needle, join yarn at beg of k row.

Row 1: Knit.

Row 2: Sl 1, p 12. Repeat last 2 rows 8 times.

Next Row: K 2, sl 1, k 1, psso, k 1, turn; sl 1, p 3, turn; k 3, sl 1, k 1 psso, k 1, turn; sl 1, p 4, turn; k 4, sl 1, k 1, psso, k 1, turn; sl 1, p 5, turn; k 5, sl 1, k 1, psso, k 1, turn; sl 1, p 6, turn; k 6, sl 1, k 1, psso, k 1—8 sts. Pick up and k 9 sts on side of right heel, k 26 sts on instep holder, pick up and k 9 sts on inner edge of left heel, k 8 sts on safety pin—60 sts.

Shape Gussets and Instep: Row 1 and All Odd Rows: Purl.

Row 2: K 14, k 2 tog, k 28, sl 1, k 1, psso, k 14.

Row 4: K 13, k 2 tog, k 28, sl 1, k 1, psso, k 13.

Row 6: K 12, k 2 tog, k 28, sl 1, k 1, psso, k 12.

Row 8: K 11, k 2 tog, k 28, sl 1, k 1, psso, k 11.

Row 10: K 10, k 2 tog, k 28, sl 1, k 1, psso, k 10.

Row 12: K 9, k 2 tog, k 28, sl 1, k 1, psso, k 9—48 sts.

Row 13: Purl.

Foot: Work in stockinette st, dec 1 st each side of next row, work even on 46 sts for 2½″, end p row.

Shape Toe: Row 1: K 9, k 2 tog, k 1, put marker on needle, k 1, sl 1, k 1, psso, k 16, k 2 tog, k 1, put marker on needle, k 1, sl 1, k 1, psso, k 9—4 sts dec. P 1 row.

Row 3: (K to within 3 sts of marker, k 2 tog, k 1, sl marker, k 1, sl 1, k 1, psso) twice, k remaining sts. Repeat last 2 rows 6 times—14 sts. Cut yarn, leave long end for sewing. Sew sole and back seam. Weave toe sts tog.

FINISHING: Steam-press stocking. Make twisted cord, chain, or fabric hanger. Sew rows of ball fringe around top of stocking.

Weave-It Stockings

SIZE: 18″ long.

MATERIALS: For holly stocking, 2 ounces red knitting worsted, ¼ yard green felt, red ball fringe. All-purpose glue. For embroidered stocking, 2 ounces white knitting worsted, small amount of red and green. 4″ Weave-It loom.

STOCKING: Make 16 squares on Weave-It loom. Sew tog on wrong side with overcast st following diagram. Round off heel and toe squares. Turn. Steam-press.

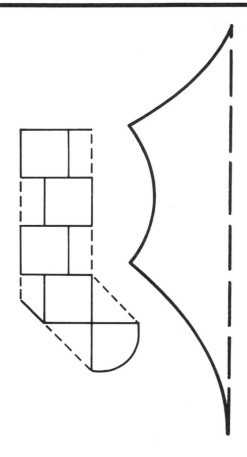

Holly Stocking: Cut 20 leaves from green felt, using pattern. Stitch each 2 leaves tog, stitching down center and around leaf, close to edge. Glue to stocking as shown. Glue red balls from fringe at top of leaf groups.

Embroidered Stocking: With red, work cross-stitches over seams. With green, work running stitch between crosses. (See Stitch Details, page 105.)

Hangers: Make red twisted cord about 8″ long (use 1 yard of yarn, double it and twist). Sew ends inside top back of stocking.

Green Crochet Stocking

SIZE: 16″ long.

MATERIALS: Knitting worsted, 4 ounces green. Wooden beads, 12 mm size, 13 natural, 13 red. Crochet hook size I. Light cardboard.

GAUGE: 4 sts = 1″ (To test gauge, see page 108.)

STOCKING:

Foot: Cut strip of cardboard ½″ wide, about 4″ long. Beg at bottom, ch 71. Sc in 2nd ch from hook and in each ch across—70 sc. Ch 1, turn each row.

Loop Row: Sc in first sc. Hold cardboard in back of work, even with top edge. Pull yarn down between work and cardboard and up in back of cardboard. Work sc in first st—loop st made. Work loop st in each sc across, sc in last sc—inc made at beg and end of row.

Sc Row: 2 sc in first sc, sc in each st across, 2 sc in last sc—74 sc. Working loop st row and sc row alternately, inc 1 st each end each row for 4 more rows—82 sts. Work even on 82 sts for 7 rows. Dec 1 st each end each row for 6 rows, end with loop row—70 sts. End off.

Leg: Row 1: With loop side facing, join yarn in 16th st, ch 1, sc in 17th st and in next 37 sts. Ch 1, turn.

Row 2: Work 38 loop sts. Work even on 38 sts until piece is about 14½″ long, or less if yarn is running out. End off. Sew seam, rounding off heel a bit.

Cuff: String beads on remaining yarn, alternating natural and red. Join yarn in first st at front seam of stocking.

Row 1: Push beads down out of way. From right side, sc in each st around, work 1 sc in seam—39 sc. Join, ch 1, turn each row.

Row 2: Sc in each sc.

Row 3: Sc in first 2 sc, * with bead in front, sc in next sc, sc in each of next 2 sc, repeat from * around, end bead sc in last sc—13 beads.

Rows 4 and 5: Sc in each sc.

Row 6: With bead in back, sc in first sc, * sc in each of next 2 sc, bead sc in next sc, repeat from * around, end sc in each of last 2 sc. Work 1 to 3 more rows of sc. End off.

Hanger: Make 7″ ch. Work 1 rows sc in ch. Sew ends of hanger inside back edge of stocking.

Looped Cuff Stocking

SIZE: 17" long.

MATERIALS: Knitting worsted, 5 ounces red, 2 ounces white. Crochet hook size I. Light cardboard.

GAUGE: 4 sc = 1". (To test gauge, see page 108.)

STOCKING: SIDE (make 2): Beg at top with red, ch 21.

Row 1: Sc in 2nd ch from hook and in each remaining ch—20 sc. Ch 1, turn each row. Work 55 more rows of 20 sc. At end of last row, ch 18. Sc in 2nd ch from hook and in next 16 ch, sc in 20 sc—37 sc. Work even for 3 more rows. At end of last row, ch 2. Sc in 2nd ch, sc across—38 sc. Repeat last 2 rows—39 sc. Work even for 5 rows. Work 2 sc tog, at toe. Work 1 row even. Repeat last 2 rows—37 sc. Work 1 more row even. Dec 1 sc at heel and every row for 3 rows. End off.

BOXING STRIP: With red, ch 5. Work as for row 1 of side. Work even on 4 sc until strip is right length to go around edge of stocking from top edge to top edge. Begin to sew strip to one side of stocking to get strip exactly right. Sew to other side, matching carefully.

CUFF: Cut strip of cardboard 4" long and ¾" wide. With white, ch 59. Work as for row 1 of side—58 sc.

Loop Row: Hold cardboard behind work with edge even with top. Bring yarn down between work and cardboard and up in back, sc in first st—loop st made. Work loop st in each sc across. Working 1 row sc, 1 row loop st, work 6 more rows. Dec 4 sc evenly across next row. Work 1 row loop st. Repeat last 2 rows once—50 loop sts. End off. Sew side edges tog forming ring. Sew to top of stocking.

Hanger: With red, make ch 7" long. Sc in 2nd ch from hook and in each ch. Sew ends inside top of stocking.

Mr. & Mrs. Santa Claus

Foam balls, bottles, pink socks, and cotton batting. Scraps of velvet, lace, and "ermine." Put it all together and presto: Mr. and Mrs. Claus.

EQUIPMENT: Pencil. Ruler. Scissors. Tracing paper. Straight pins. Small knife. Sewing needle. Sewing machine. Compass.

MATERIALS: For each: Glass bottle with narrow neck, about 10" tall. Plastic foam ball, 3" diameter. Adult size, medium weight pink sock. Large scrap red velvet. Scraps black and pink felt. Tiny pink pompon from ball fringe. Cotton batting. Red, pink, and white sewing thread. White glue. Masking tape. For Mrs. Santa: Lace, 1" wide, 2⅛ yards, or use ruffled lace trim, 1" wide, 1⅜ yards. Eyelet scrap, 12" × 6". Decorative white trims: ½" wide, 21½" long for apron tie; ⅜" wide, 6" long for neck trim. Gray sewing thread. Heavy gray yarn for hair. One-half plastic foam oval for bun, about 2" × 3½". Thin black wire for glasses. Small scrap paper for list. For Mr. Santa: Black velvet ribbon, ⅝" wide, ⅝ yard. Scraps white fake fur. Scrap black leather or leather-like fabric, 2" wide and long enough to fit around base of bottle. Jingle bell. Small gold buckle.

GENERAL DIRECTIONS: Using sharp pencil, draw lines across pattern connecting grid lines. Enlarge pattern by copying on paper ruled in ½″ squares. (See Enlarging the Pattern, page 103). Trace patterns; complete half-patterns indicated by dash lines. Insert top of bottle halfway into plastic foam ball, using knife to hollow out.

Pull sock over bottle and ball; pin toe of sock to top of ball. (Add stuffing to Mrs. Santa; see below.) Glue edges of sock to bottom of bottle, pulling sock down evenly. Cut black felt circle slightly smaller than bottom of bottle, and glue to bottom, covering edges of sock.

Use patterns to cut two pairs of hands from pink felt, small for Mrs. Santa and large for Mr. Santa. Stitch each pair together close to raw edges.

MRS. SANTA: Before gluing edges of sock to bottom of bottle, stuff heel of sock with cotton batting for derrière; stuff opposite side of sock above heel for bosom. Place small amounts of glue on bottle and batting to prevent shifting.

To Make Face: Cut two ¼″-diameter circles from black felt for eyes and glue to front of ball (on side above bosom); separate a small section of the gray yarn into plies and cut 1″ length of fine yarn; cut length in half and glue pieces over eyes for eyebrows; glue on pink pompon for nose; cut and glue curved pink felt piece for mouth. For hair, cut about fifty 12″ lengths of gray yarn and a 7″ strip of masking tape. Arrange yarn pieces side by side on sticky side of tape, centered crosswise and with long edges flush. Cover length of tape, then machine-stitch yarn down lengthwise center of tape with gray thread for "part" in hair. Glue tape to top of head, about 1½″ above eyebrows. Dab glue on yarn and arrange hair smoothly around face and as shown in photograph, keeping edges of yarn flush. Tie gray thread around neck to hold ends of yarn in place. For bun, cover plastic foam oval lengthwise, then crosswise, with gray yarn, keeping edges flush and gluing yarn in place. Glue oval horizontally across back of head near the top. Braid nine strips of yarn to fit around base of oval; glue in place. For

glasses, cut three lengths of wire, two 1½″ long and one 6″ long. Following Figure 1, bend 6″ length into two circles; bend 1½″ lengths around circles for earpieces. Place glasses on nose; run earpieces under hair.

To Make Dress: Cut piece of red velvet 20″ wide; for length, measure from Mrs. Santa's neck to bottom of bottle, adding 1″ to measurement. With right sides facing, stitch short ends together ¼″ from raw edges. Finish long edges by turning ¼″ to wrong side and stitching in place. Machine-baste 40″ of lace and gather same length as one finished edge of dress, or cut pre-gathered lace trim to fit; pin and stitch to wrong side of velvet for bottom of dress. Using red thread, machine-baste ¼″ and again 2″ from other finished edge. Pull dress over bottle; pull bobbin threads to gather fabric around neck, and again below padded bosom. Tie threads to secure gathers. Sew white neck trim to top of dress and to sock with invisible stitches.

To Make Apron: Turn one long edge and two short edges of eyelet piece ¼″ to wrong side and stitch in place. Gather 24″ of lace same length as finished long edge of eyelet, or cut the ruffled lace to fit; pin and stitch to right side. Machine-baste other long edge and gather to length of 5½″. Center gathered edge on 21½″ length of white apron trim, and stitch trim over gathered edge. Tie apron around waist.

To Make Arms: Cut 15″ × 3½″ piece of velvet. Turn short raw edges ¼″ to wrong side and stitch. Add lace ruffle to finished edges in same manner as for dress. Make a tube by stitching long sides together with right sides facing, ¼″ from raw edges. Turn tube right side out and fold so seam is centered on one side. Glue wrists of pink felt hands inside tube so hands protrude, but leaving ends of tube open. Loosely stuff cotton batting into tube for 4″ at each end. Tie red thread around tube about 1″ away from each end for cuff. Tack center of tube to back of Mrs. Santa's neck, with seam facing inward. Cut 1″ × 2½″ strip of paper. Scribble some lines on one side to simulate writing. Bring arms to front and pin hands together and to list with straight pin.

MR. SANTA: For boots, glue leather or leather-like strip around base of bottle, with one long edge flush with bottom edge of bottle, and short edges overlapping. Cut 15″ × 4″ piece from red velvet for pants. With right sides facing, stitch short edges together, making ¼″ seam; turn to right side. Turn both long edges under ¼″ and stitch; machine-baste ¼″ away from each finished edge. Slip pants over bottle so edges of pants and boots meet. Pull bobbin thread to gather bottom edge of pants to fit snugly around bottle; glue to bottle. Stuff pants evenly with batting. Gather top edge of pants and slip-stitch to sock. Cut 1″-wide strip of fake fur to cover edges where pants and boots meet; glue in place.

For Jacket: Cut 20″ × 7″ piece from red velvet. With right sides facing, stitch short edges together making ¼″ seam; turn to right side. Turn both long edges under ¼″ and stitch; machine-baste ¼″ from one finished edge for neck. Cut 6½″ × 1″ strip of fake fur and glue over seamline for front of jacket. Cut 18½″ × 1″ fur strip and glue around bottom of jacket with top edge flush with edges of front fur strip. Slip jacket over bottle; pull bobbin thread to gather neck edge to fit top of bottle, and tie thread to secure gathers. Stuff jacket with batting loosely in back and fully in front to give Santa a round belly. Make belt using small gold buckle and black velvet ribbon; slip-stitch to jacket at each side.

To Make Arms: Proceed in same manner as for Mrs. Santa, cutting 17″ × 4″ strip of red velvet and gluing 4″ × 1″ strip of fake fur around each cuff. Secure pink felt hands and stuff ends of tube as for Mrs. Santa; pin center of tube to back of jacket with seamed side facing inward. Slip-stitch arms to belt at sides just above cuffs.

For Face: Cut two ¼″ circles from black felt for eyes and glue in place; glue on pink

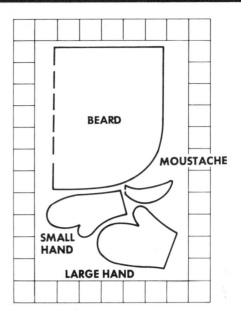

FIGURE 1

pompon for nose. For fringe of hair, cut 7″ × 2″ piece from fur and glue lengthwise to back of head just above top edge of jacket. Use patterns to cut moustache and beard from fur; glue beard to face just under nose; glue moustache to top of beard.

To Make Hat: Cut triangle from red velvet, 12″ at base and 6″ high. Stitch short sides together, right sides facing and with ¼″ seams. Turn in bottom edge ¼″ and stitch. Make pompon by cutting 2″-diameter circle from fake fur. Machine-baste all around close to raw edge; pull bobbin thread to gather fabric until it fits tightly over tip of hat. Slip-stitch pompon in place. Stitch jingle bell to base of pompon. Cut 1″-wide fur strip to fit around base of hat; glue over finished edge. Glue edges of hat to Santa's head.

Cross-Stitched Gingham Set

*Counted cross-stitch on crisp gingham brings holiday spirit to the table:
place mats and tablecloth, a basket of quilted poinsettias for the
centerpiece and a matching apron and potholder set.*

Poinsettia Centerpiece

SIZE: Approximately 15″ wide, 9″ high.

EQUIPMENT: Pencil. Ruler. Tape measure. Tracing paper. Scissors. X-acto knife. Large compass, or string and thumbtack. Masking tape. Knitting needle. Straight pins. Sewing needles. Sewing machine. Iron. Thin stiff cardboard, 4″ × 8″.

MATERIALS: Illustration board, one sheet 30″ × 40″. Gingham fabric with small checks 45″ wide: 1 yard each of red and green; ⅓ yard brown. Sewing thread to match fabric. Yellow ball fringe, with ½″ balls, enough to cut 9 balls. Polyester fiberfill. All-purpose white glue.

DIRECTIONS:

To Make a String Compass: Cut string about 5″ longer than radius of circle or arc you wish to draw. Tie one end of string to pencil near point. Stretch string taut and tie a knot at other end so distance between pencil and knot equals length of radius. Thumbtack knot at center point of circle you wish to draw. Holding pencil perpendicular to drawing surface, swing pencil around to mark a circle or arc as directed.

To Make Pattern: Trace actual-size half-pattern, completing leaf/petal by reversing it for other side. Glue tracing to cardboard and cut out when dry.

Basket: Using large compass or string compass, mark on illustration board near one corner, one 4⅛″-radius circle and two 5⅜″-radius circles. Using opposite corner of illustration board as center point, mark two arcs from one side edge to adjacent side edge with radii of 17½″ and 22½″. Cut out circles and 5″ band between arcs with X-acto knife. Bend wide edge of band around one larger (top) circle, matching edges and taping together as you work around; lap and tape ends. Working as for top, tape free edge of band around smaller (bottom) circle.

Lid: Using second large circle as pattern, mark a circle 2″ in from one corner of green

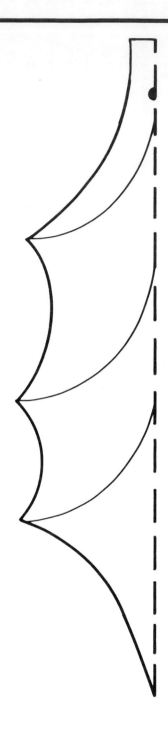

To Cover Sides: Using a row of checks as a guide, cut brown gingham in half lengthwise. With right sides facing and edges even, stitch strips together ¼″ in from one short edge, for one 6″ × 90″ strip. Turn short ends ¼″ to wrong side and stitch. Baste piece ¾″ in from each long edge. Fit around basket sides, pulling both sets of basting threads until fabric fits top and bottom edges of basket; secure threads, remove piece, and topstitch gathers. Fringe top and bottom edges by pulling lengthwise threads from four rows of checks. Place piece around basket matching edges; glue to basket and whipstitch short ends together.

Leaves and Petals: Make 12 leaves from green gingham and 18 petals from red gingham, as follows: Fold fabric in half to form two thicknesses with right side inward. Using pattern, mark designated number of pieces on doubled fabric, spacing them ½″ apart; cut out ¼″ beyond marked outlines (seamline). Stitch pairs together with right sides facing and raw edges even, making ¼″ seams and leaving bottom straight edge open; clip into seam allowance at curves; turn to right side; press. Stuff lightly and evenly, poking fiberfill into points with knitting needle. Referring to pattern, machine-stitch veins and down center (dash line) to dot, through all thicknesses as shown.

To Assemble: For each poinsettia, gather together six red petals at their bases; secure by tightly winding thread around bases; spread petals evenly to form flower. Glue or stitch three yellow balls from fringe to center of poinsettia, as shown in photograph. Visually divide cushioned lid into thirds; slip-stitch one poinsettia to each section of lid. Arrange leaves around poinsettias; slip-stitch in place.

gingham, on wrong side; cut out, adding 2″ beyond circle edge. With long hand or machine stitches, baste all around fabric ¼″ in from edge; pull thread to gather slightly, forming "pouch." Stuff lightly with fiberfill. Add cardboard circle, tucking fiberfill around edges. Pull thread to tighten fabric over circle; secure with several small back stitches. Tape or glue raw edges to circle. Glue lid to top of basket.

Gingham Set

SIZES: Tea cloth, 42″ × 44″; four place mats, each 13¾″ × 18″; pot holder, 6½″ × 7¼″; apron, adult size.

EQUIPMENT: Pencil. Ruler. Tailor's chalk. Sewing and embroidery needles. Embroidery hoop. Scissors. Sewing machine. Steam iron. Padded surface.

MATERIALS: Cotton or cotton-blend fabric, 45″ wide: green gingham with ⅛″ checks; solid red, solid white. Rickrack, ½″ wide, green, red. (See chart for all yardage amounts.) Six-strand embroidery floss: white, 1 skein for each project; crimson, emerald, 4 skeins each for tea cloth or placemats; 2 skeins each for apron; 1 skein each for pot holder. Green, red thread. Batting for pot holder. (**Note:** If making tea cloth, apron, and potholder, do not buy extra gingham fabric for apron and pot holder because pieces may be cut from tea cloth scrap.)

	Tea Cloth	Mats	Apron	Pot Holder
Gingham	1¼	1⅛	⅓	scrap
Red	1¼	1⅝	¾	scrap
White	—	⅞	—	—
Green rickrack	4⅛	4½	1⅔	⅔
Red rickrack	4⅔	6½	1⅔	¼

GENERAL DIRECTIONS: See Embroidery for embroidery tips and Stitch Details on pages 104 and 105. Embroider design for each piece on gingham in cross-stitch, following chart and color key. Each square on chart represents one gingham check; each symbol on chart represents one cross-stitch worked over one check. Gingham checks are not perfectly square and usually run 8 checks per inch (cpi) in one direction and 7 checks per inch in the other on ⅛″ check fabric. To begin embroidery, place gingham piece so that the 8 cpi edges are at top and bottom and 7 cpi edges are at sides. Mark top. Starting in upper right corner of piece, measure down and in as directed to nearest white check, for first cross-stitch; continue across to the left. Embroider all red and green cross-stitches on white checks and all white cross-stitches on green checks. Steam-press finished embroidery gently on padded surface.

When embroidery is completed, cut out

gingham piece as directed. Assemble piece with red fabric, trimming with rickrack. Make seams ¼″ wide (or two rows of squares), unless otherwise directed.

TEA CLOTH: Measure 2¼″ down and 3″ in for first check; embroider with red cross-stitch for corner stitch. Complete corner motif from A to A (8 green stitches, 4 red stitches, 1 white stitch). Continuing across top, work section between A and C 12 times, then work A/B section once. Return to upper right corner. For right edge, work A/C section 11 times and A/B section once. Turn chart as necessary to work adjacent corners, then work border design along remaining two edges and fourth corner in same manner.

Cut out gingham piece, leaving 11 rows of checks around outer edge of embroidery and 6 rows of checks around inner edge; piece will not be perfectly square. Measure ½″ away from the outer edge of embroidery and pin red rickrack in place all around, easing at corners; there should be two rows of squares between embroidery and inner points of rickrack. Slip-stitch in place, turning raw ends under where they meet. Press inner edges of gingham ¼″ to wrong side, clipping fabric at corners.

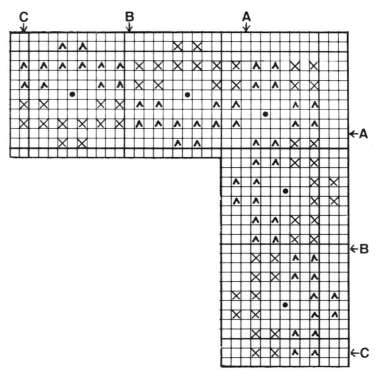

With right side of gingham facing wrong side of red fabric, pin gingham border to red piece, trimming red fabric to size. Stitch pieces together around outer edges. Trim seams, clip corners at an angle, and turn gingham to right side; press so seam is not visible on right side. Pin green rickrack over inner pressed edges of gingham and slip-stitch in place, securing gingham to red piece.

PLACE MATS: Cut gingham fabric in half lengthwise and crosswise for four equal pieces. For each mat, measure 2¾" down and 2¾" in for first stitch. Work embroidery design around gingham in same manner as for tea cloth; for top edges, work section between A and C four times and A/B section once; for side edges, work section A/C twice and A/B once. Cut out gingham piece and slip-stitch red rickrack in place as for tea cloth; press raw inner edges ¼" to wrong side. Make four.

Cut eight pieces from solid red fabric, each 14¼" × 18½", or size of gingham pieces. Cut four pieces from white, each 13¾" × 18". Sandwich each white piece, centered, between layers of red fabric and baste around edges, making four backings. Mark parallel lines across length of each backing, spacing lines about 2" apart. Stitch on marked lines to quilt. Assemble mats as for tea cloth.

POT HOLDER: Use scrap of gingham about 7" square. Measure 2" down and 1" in for first green cross-stitch (lower right in diagonal row). Complete corner motif and continue across top, to center of piece. Repeat chart in reverse to upper left, omitting center row marked with arrow. Returning to upper right,

work right side in same manner. Complete border design along remaining two edges and fourth corner in same manner. Cut out gingham piece, leaving five rows of checks around outer edge of embroidery.

Cut one strip of gingham 1" × 4½" for hanger; cut two pieces from red fabric, each 7" × 7¾"; cut batting 6½" × 7¼". Press long raw edges of gingham strip ¼" to wrong side, then press strip in half lengthwise with raw edges inward; top-stitch pressed edges together. Fold strip in half crosswise, matching ends, then stitch to corner of one red piece on right side, matching raw edges. Baste batting, centered, to wrong side of one red piece. Stitch red pieces together with right sides facing and loop in between; leave opening for turning. Turn to right side; fold raw edges in; slip-stitch opening closed.

Press raw edges of gingham piece ¼" to wrong side; pin to one side of red piece, leaving equal margins around edges. Count four rows of checks inside inner edge of embroidery and machine-stitch gingham to pot holder on this line, forming a square; remove basting from pot holder. Pin red rickrack over machine-stitched square and slip-stitch in place. Pin green rickrack over pressed edges of gingham and slip-stitch in place.

APRON: Mark the following strips on gingham so that 8 cpi are along the length of each strip: 3¾" × 32" hem border, 5½" × 18¾" waistband, and 3¼" × 5¾" pocket facing. Do not cut out pieces. With long edges of hem border as top and bottom, measure 1¼" down and ¾" in from upper right corner of marked strip to nearest white check; work first red cross-stitch at upper right of border motif. Continue working across gingham, embroidering section between A and C 10 times, then A/B section once. Slip-stitch red rickrack 1" above and parallel to bottom edge; there should be two rows of squares between embroidery and inner points of rickrack. Position pocket border and waistband with long edges as top and bottom. For pocket border, measure 1¾" down and ¾" in from upper right corner to nearest white check for first red cross-stitch; work pattern as shown.

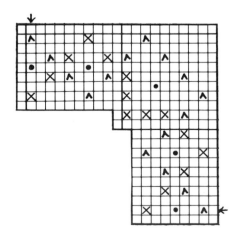

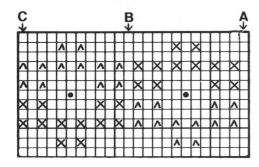

C   B   A

For waistband, measure 4″ down and ⅝″ in from upper right corner to nearest white check for first green cross-stitch at A; work in pattern from A to B across fabric to within 2 checks at opposite end. Measure ½″ above embroidery on waistband and pocket border; slip-stitch red rickrack in place at this measurement, leaving two rows of checks between embroidery and rickrack. Cut out gingham pieces on marked lines; press long raw edges opposite rickrack under ¼″.

From red fabric, cut one skirt 32″ × 20″, one pocket 6″ × 5¾″, and two ties, each 26″ × 2¾″. For hem, stitch bottom long edge of gingham hem border to skirt with right side of gingham facing wrong side of skirt and raw edges even; press gingham to right side. Pin, then slip-stitch green rickrack over pressed edge of gingham border, attaching it to skirt. Press raw side edges of skirt ¼″ then again ¼″

to wrong side; topstitch in place. For pocket, with right side of gingham facing wrong side of pocket and raw edges even; stitch 5¾″ edges of pocket and top edge of border together. Fold border over to right side of pocket; slip-stitch green rickrack over pressed edge of gingham, attaching border to pocket. Press raw edges of pocket ¼″ to wrong side and pin to skirt so top of pocket is 6″ below top of skirt and away from left side edge; topstitch in place ⅛″ away from pressed edges of pocket.

Baste across upper edge of skirt; gather to fit raw edge of gingham waistband. Stitch waistband to skirt with right sides facing, adjusting gathers to fit. Press long raw edges and one short edge of each tie ⅛″ then again ⅛″ to wrong side; stitch to secure. Fold finished end of each tie to the wrong side on a diagonal; slip-stitch to secure, making a pointed end. With right sides facing, stitch tie to each end of waistband so bottom edge of tie touches seamline of skirt and waistband; baste in place. With right side inward, fold waistband in half with ties in between; stitch side edges. Trim seams; clip corners; turn to right side and press. Slip-stitch pressed edge of waistband in place, covering seam allowance. On right side, pin, then slip-stitch green rickrack over seamline of waistband and skirt.

B   A

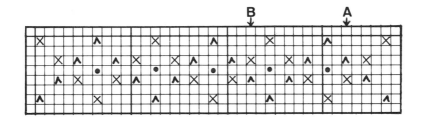

P A R T III
FILLING THE STOCKINGS

The children's eyes will really sparkle when they spy these great gifts and stocking stuffers. All sorts of irresistible cuddly creatures are ready to add to the festivities: snowmen who will never melt, a traveling bear family with its own fold-up house, a lion puppet, a pig, and a panda, a Santa or two, Humpty-Dumpty, and a raft of dolls. There are also special gifts for the new baby, and some novelty stockings for the older set.

Celebrate Baby's first Christmas with something special: bibs decorated with machine appliqué and embroidery, little cross-stitched stockings trimmed in eyelet, or an enchanting snowman family.

Cross-Stitch Stockings (See photograph, page 69).

SIZE: 10½" long.

EQUIPMENT: Pencil. Ruler. Scissors. Masking tape. Embroidery hoop and needle. Sewing machine. Straight pin. Steam iron.

MATERIALS:

For Each: Even-weave fabric such as Aida or hardanger cloth, 22 threads-to-the-inch, 9" × 12" piece. Pearl cotton #8, one ball each of the following colors: pink, green, yellow, blue, orange, red, and black (for train stocking only). Felt, 9" × 12" piece red or green. Double-fold bias tape, ¼" wide, 1 yard red or green. White eyelet trim, 1" wide, ⅜ yard. Sewing thread to match fabric and felt.

DIRECTIONS: Read Cross-Stitch How-To's and see stitch detail. (See also Embroidery on page 104.) With short edges of fabric at top and bottom, measure 3" down and 2" in from upper right corner for placement of first stitch, indicated on charts by arrows; mark mesh with a pin. Insert fabric in hoop. Follow How-To's, stitch details, Color Key, and chart to stitch design in cross-stitch; stars are worked in straight stitches, each over two fabric threads.

After all embroidery is completed, remove fabric from hoop; steam-press lightly on wrong side. Using pencil, lightly mark stocking shape on wrong side of fabric; see illustration and count meshes from chart. Cut out stocking ¼" from marked line; use as pattern

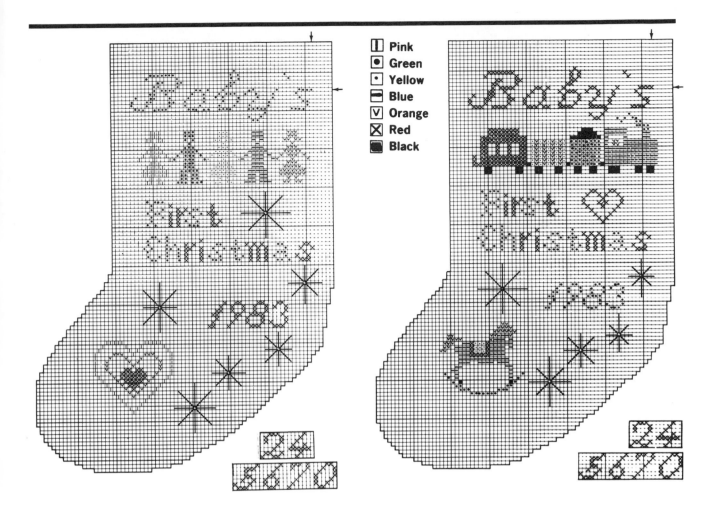

Legend:
- ☐ Pink
- ⊙ Green
- ⋅ Yellow
- ⊟ Blue
- V Orange
- ⊠ Red
- ■ Black

to cut backing from desired color felt. With right sides facing and edges even, stitch pieces together, making ¼″ seams and leaving top edge open. Turn top edge under ¼″; press. Cut 11″ length of red or green bias tape. Starting at center back of stocking, encase top edge in tape, turning under lapped end of tape ¼″. Slip-stitch in place on inside and outside of stocking. Cut 11″ length of eyelet trim. Starting at center back of stocking, slip-stitch top of trim to inside edge of stocking so that scalloped edge extends upward as shown; lap ends as for bias tape. For hanger, cut 9″ length of matching bias tape; turn ends under ¼″. Fold tape in half widthwise; slip-stitch folded ends to right back edge of felt, leaving loop free.

CROSS-STITCH HOW-TO'S: To prevent fabric from raveling, bind all raw edges with masking tape, whipstitch edges by hand, or machine-stitch ⅛″ in from all edges. Work embroidery in a frame or hoop to keep fabric

taut; move hoop as needed. Cut yarn into 18″ lengths. To begin a strand, leave an end on back and work over it to secure; to end, run needle under four or five stitches on back of work.

Each symbol on chart represents one cross-stitch worked over two horizontal and two vertical fabric threads; each blank square on chart represents two unworked threads. Different symbols represent different colors. When working cross-stitches, work all underneath stitches in one direction and all top stitches in the opposite direction, making sure all strands lie smooth and flat; allow needle to hang freely from work occasionally, to untwist floss. Make crosses touch by inserting needle in same hole used for adjacent stitch (see stitch detail).

Cross-Stitch

Snowman Family (See photograph, page 69.)

SIZE: Frosty, 9″ tall. Holly, 7¾″ tall. Candy, 4½″ tall.

EQUIPMENT: Sharp colored pencil. Ruler. Pencil. Paper for patterns. Tracing paper. Scissors. Pinking shears. Straight pins. Compass. Fine paintbrush. Sewing needle. Sewing machine. Steam/dry iron. Sprayer bottle filled with water.

MATERIALS: One pair men's white cotton socks, size 10. One pair boy's white cotton socks, size 7. Polyester fiberfill. Household string. Lightweight and heavyweight cardboard. Felt: 9″ × 12″ pieces, one black and one green, and scraps of white, pink and red. Scraps of cotton fabric: holly print, 12″ square; red polka dot, 6″ square; solid red, 12″ square. Scrap of fusible interfacing. Satin ribbon: green, ⅜″ wide, ½ yard; white, ⅝″ wide, ¼ yard. White lace trim, ⅜″ wide, ½ yard. Scrap of gold cord. Sewing thread: red, white, green, and black. Eight red beads, ³⁄₁₆″ wide. White acrylic paint. Pipe cleaner (or chenille stem), 6½″ long. White pompon, 1¼″ in diameter. White glue.

GENERAL DIRECTIONS: Using sharp colored pencil and a ruler, draw lines across patterns, connecting grid lines. Enlarge patterns by copying on paper ruled in ½″ squares (See Enlarging the Pattern, page 103); complete half patterns indicated by long dash lines. Trace patterns and cut out; use to mark pieces on wrong side of designated fabrics. Cut out pieces on marked lines, unless otherwise directed. Stitch pieces together, making ¼″ seams and using matching thread, unless otherwise indicated.

To Make Body: For Frosty and Holly, cut arm and body pieces from one man's sock for each, following diagram; discard heel and cuff sections. For Candy, cut off toe section from two boy's socks just below the heel as for large dolls; discard upper sections; for arm pieces, cut one toe section in half lengthwise. Set arm pieces aside.

Using fiberfill, firmly stuff body pieces to about 7″ long for Frosty and Holly, 3½″ for Candy. Using string, tie off toe end to make

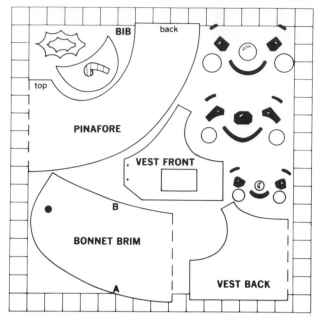

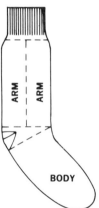

Cutting Diagram for Large Dolls

head, 2½″ from end for Frosty, 3″ for Holly, and 1½″ for Candy.

For each base, draw two circles on heavy cardboard using compass, 3¼″ in diameter for large dolls and 2″ in diameter for Candy. Holding stuffed sock head down, insert one circle into the body on top of the stuffing so that it forms a level bottom and sock extends about 1½″ beyond it. Fold down top edge of sock all around and glue to circle; pinch up any fullness and trim with scissors so that glued edge lies flat. Glue one side of remaining circle to black felt; trim off excess; glue other side to base, aligning edges with edges of circle inside body.

To make arm patterns, draw two rectangles on lightweight cardboard, one 3″ × 1½″ and one 1¾″ × 1¼″; cut out, rounding corners of one short side on each. Unfold arm pieces cut from sock and refold with wrong side out. Using large arm pattern for Frosty and Holly, and small pattern for Candy, place one long side of pattern on fold and trace outline around three sides. Trim away excess sock to within ¼″ of outline. Machine-stitch along two sides, leaving short straight (top) side open. Turn seams to inside and loosely stuff arm with fiberfill; turn top edge ¼″ to inside and slip-stitch closed. Slip-stitch arms to sides of body, using color illustration as a guide for placement.

To Make Face: Following color illustration for color and placement and using patterns given, cut individual features from felt and glue in position. Using brush and white acrylic paint, add highlights to eyes and nose following pattern.

FROSTY: Make body and face following General Directions. From green felt, cut one vest back, one pocket, and two vest fronts. Pin vest front pieces to vest back matching sides and shoulders; stitch, making ³⁄₁₆″ seams. Press seams open and turn to inside. Using double strand of white thread and running stitch, stitch pocket to right vest front; stitch buttons to left vest front at dots. Place vest on snowman, overlapping fronts as shown, and tack together invisibly from underside.

To make bow tie, cut two strips of polka dot fabric, one 3¼″ × 2½″ and one 1½″ × 1″. Fold the larger strip lengthwise with wrong side out and raw edges even. Stitch edges together along two sides, leaving one short side open for turning. Clip seam allowance at corners and turn. Fold raw edge at opening ¼″ to inside and slip-stitch closed. Double-fold remaining strip widthwise to a ½″ width, press. Wrap strip lengthwise around larger piece and draw it up into a bow-tie shape; overlap ends of smaller strip in back and slip-stitch together. Stitch back of tie to neck as shown. Cut and fold scrap of fabric for hanky; insert in pocket.

From black felt, cut two circles 5″ in diameter for top and bottom of hat brim; cut out a 2½″-diameter circle from the center of each. For crown, cut a strip 9¾″ × 2½″ and a circle 3½″ in diameter. Stitch short edges of strip together forming a cylinder, then stitch one edge to edge of circle; stitch remaining edge to inside edge of one brim piece so that all seams are facing. Trim seams and turn hat right side out. Push remaining brim piece down around hat, pulling crown through center hole; pin brims together with outside edges even; stitch all around outside edges. Trim seam allowance and turn second brim to inside to complete hat. Using sprayer bottle, lightly mist hat with water and crush lightly for "old" look; let dry. From lightweight cardboard, cut a strip 8″ × 1½″. Curl into a ring and insert into crown of hat to support sides. From holly print fabric, cut a 9½″ × 2″ strip for hatband. Double-fold strip lengthwise to a ¾″ width and glue around hat as shown, overlapping ends in back; turn lapped end under ¼″ and slip-stitch in place. Using small holly leaf pattern, cut nine holly leaves from green felt and glue in a cluster on hatband. Sew three red beads in center for berries and glue hat on doll's head in position shown. Bend pipe cleaner into a "cane." Cut a 7″ × ¾″ strip of black felt and fold it lengthwise around cane to cover completely. Whipstitch raw edges together along length and glue cane to Frosty's hand as shown.

HOLLY: Make body and face following General Directions. Using pattern, cut two bonnet brim pieces from red fabric and two from fusible interfacing, adding ¼″ seam allowances. Place raw edges even and fuse one piece of interfacing to the wrong side of each fabric piece. Place right sides of fabric pieces together and stitch along seamline of edge "A." Trim seam allowance and turn to the inside. Along edge "B", turn raw edges ¼″ to inside and press. Cut a circle 7″ in diameter from red fabric for bonnet back. Measure in 1″ from outside edge and cut a straight line through circle to make a straight bottom edge. Baste curved edge and gather to fit brim edge "B"; insert gathered edge ¼″ into brim between layers, and slip-stitch in place on each side. Turn straight bottom edge ⅛″ to wrong side twice; hem. Baste ⅛″ in from hem; do not end off. Place bonnet on doll's head and pull basting to gather, to fit doll's head. Take a few backstitches and cut thread.

Remove bonnet from doll. Cut two 9″ pieces of green ribbon. Fold one end of each under ½″ and tack one to each side of bonnet at dot for tie. Fold ½ yard of white ribbon into several loops 1½″ long and fan loops to form a bow; tack as needed to hold shape. From green felt, cut 12 holly leaves using large leaf pattern. Stitch cluster of about seven leaves on top of bow and sew two red beads in center for berries. Replace bonnet on doll's head and tie ribbon under chin. Tack remaining leaves in a cluster at front of head as shown. Sew three beads at center for berries.

From holly print fabric, cut one pinafore, adding ¼″ seam allowances. Cut two 11″ × ¾″ bias strips for ties. With right sides out, fold strips in half lengthwise and press. Fold long raw edges of each strip ⅛″ to inside to make a tie ¼″ wide; press. Fold straight edges at top and back of pinafore ⅛″ to wrong side twice and slip-stitch. Starting at a back edge and allowing ¼″ of strip to overhang, insert raw edge of one waist/armhole between folded edges of one strip and stitch through all thicknesses close to edge. Continue stitching beyond armhole to finish tie. Repeat on other side for second tie. Fold overhanging ends of ties to wrong side and stitch. Place pinafore on doll and tie a bow at back of neck. Overlap edges of pinafore in back, adjusting to fit body, and tack together invisibly from underside.

For Handbag: Cut two 2¼″ × 1½″ strips each from red fabric and fusible interfacing. With right sides facing, stitch one long edge of one interfacing piece to one long edge of fabric piece; trim seam allowance, turn seam to inside and fuse interfacing to wrong side of fabric; repeat for second set. With fabric sides facing and stitched (top) edges even, stitch fused pieces together around sides and bottom, rounding corners. Trim seam allowances and turn to inside. Using small leaf pattern, cut four holly leaves from green felt and glue inside opening of handbag as shown. Sew ends of a 3½″ piece of gold cord to each side on inside for handle and glue to Holly's hand as shown.

CANDY: Make body and face following General Directions. From green felt cut bib piece and pink around bottom edge. Cut candy cane from white felt and glue to front of bib as shown. Using a double strand of red thread and long straight stitches, stitch stripes across candy cane and topstitch pinked edge in running stitch as shown (see Stitch Details, page 105). Glue bib to body front. To make beret, cut two circles from red felt, each 3½″ in diameter. From center of one piece cut out circle 2½″ in diameter to form ring. Place the two pieces together with outside edges even; stitch ¼″ from outside edge all around. Trim seam allowance and turn to inside to make beret. Stitch white pompon to center of crown and slip-stitch beret to doll's head all around.

Baby Bibs (See photograph, page 70.)

SIZES: Small bibs, 10¼″ × 12¼″; large bib, 21″ long.

EQUIPMENT: Sharp colored pencil. Pencil. Ruler. Scissors. Dressmaker's tracing (carbon) paper. Dry ball-point pen. Straight pins. Sewing and embroidery needles. Sewing machine with zigzag attachment. Iron. Knitting needle.

MATERIALS:

For Noël Bib: Two pieces white fabric 11″ × 13″, one terry cloth (or use guest towel), one cotton. White pre-gathered eyelet trim ¾″ wide, 1¼ yards. White double-fold wide bias tape, 1⅛ yards. Red and green sewing thread.

For Christmas Ball Bib: Two pieces cotton fabric 11″ × 13″, one white, one red. Fabric scraps: solid green, novelty print with Christmas motif about 4″ square (see color photograph). Batting. Light green sewing thread. Decorative print double-fold wide bias tape, 2¼ yards.

For Holly Bib: Two pieces cotton fabric 11″ × 13″, one red/green/white striped, one white. Scraps of green and red cotton fabric. Batting. Red double-fold wide bias tape, 2¼ yards. Light green sewing thread.

For Jack-in-the-Box Bib: Terry cloth, 45″ wide, ½ yard white (or use hand towel). White-dotted red cotton fabric, 36″ wide, ½ yard (or 3½ yards wide double-fold bias tape and scrap of fabric to match). Small amount of red-dotted white fabric. Felt scraps: green, yellow, pale pink, white. Six-strand embroidery floss: blue, black, red. Scrap narrow red rickrack. One Velcro® tab. Fiberfill.

For Each Bib: Sewing thread to match fabric.

GENERAL DIRECTIONS: Using sharp colored pencil, draw lines across patterns, connecting grid lines. Enlarge each pattern by copying on paper ruled in 1″ squares (See Enlarging the Pattern, page 103). Using dressmaker's carbon and dry ball-point pen, transfer each pattern to designated fabric or felt, placing long dash line of main bib pieces on fold of doubled fabric. Transfer machine embroidery lines, indicated by short dash lines. Cut out appliqué pieces ¼″ from marked lines; cut other pieces on line. Make bibs as directed below. See Appliqué, page 103.

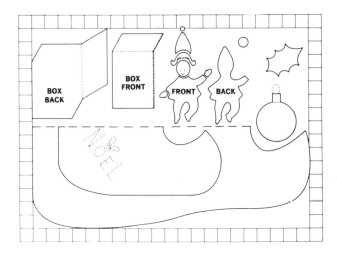

To Bind Raw Edges: With right sides facing and raw edges even, pin one long edge of bias tape to raw edge of fabric; stitch in place along first fold line. Fold tape over, enclosing raw edges of fabric, and slip-stitch opposite folded edge to back of bib. Turn under short raw edges at ends; slip-stitch in place.

NOËL BIB: Read General Directions. Use small bib pattern to cut front from white terry cloth and back from white cotton; transfer embroidery lines to terry. Set sewing machine

for close zigzag stitch. Using green thread for "Noël" and holly leaves, and red thread for berries, machine-embroider over dash lines, filling in holly. With right sides facing and raw edges even, pin eyelet trim around bib front (omitting neck edge); stitch in place. With right sides facing and eyelet trim in between, stitch bib back to front, leaving neck edge open. Turn bib to right side. With center of 40″ length of bias tape at center of neck edge, bind neck edge following General Directions and leaving ends free for ties; slip-stitch long edges of ties closed.

CHRISTMAS BALL BIB: Read General Directions. Use small bib pattern to cut front from red cotton and back from white cotton. Also cut the following appliqué pieces: two green holly leaves and Christmas ball cut from novelty fabric, centering pattern over one motif (see color photograph). Use bib pattern to cut layer of batting same size. Sandwich batting between bib front and back; stitch in place all around, ¼″ from edge. Using light green thread, machine-appliqué ball and holly to bib front, following illustration for placement. After all pieces have been appliquéd, machine-embroider over dash lines, using close zigzag stitch for hanger and medium zigzag stitch for top of circle. Bind bib edges with decorative bias tape, binding neck edge separately and making ties as for Noël Bib.

HOLLY BIB: Read General Directions. Use small bib pattern to cut front from striped cotton (with stripes running vertically) and bib back from white cotton. Also cut the following appliqué pieces: two green leaves and three red berries. Use bib pattern to cut layer of batting same size. Sandwich batting between bib front and back; stitch in place all around, ¼″ from edge. Using light green thread for leaves and red thread for berries, machine-appliqué holly to bib front, following illustration for placement. Bind bib edges with red bias tape, binding neck edge separately and making ties as for Noël Bib.

JACK-IN-THE-BOX BIB: Read General Directions. Use large pattern to cut bib from white terry cloth. Cut the following appliqué pieces: box front from white-dotted fabric, box back from red-dotted fabric; reversing pattern, cut another box front from red-dotted fabric.

Cutting on the bias, cut 1¾"-wide strips of white-dotted fabric; piece as necessary to make strip 10′ long. Fold strip in half lengthwise; press. (Note: Purchased bias tape may be substituted.)

Using red thread, appliqué box back to bib, following photograph for placement. Cut 12" length of bias tape from prepared strip; stitch edges together. On box back, machine-embroider lid "crease" following dash line and catching one end of tape in "crease." With right sides facing and raw edges even, stitch two box fronts together along upper rim, making ⅛" seam; turn to right side. Machine-embroider "corner" and upper rim, following dash lines. With red side up, appliqué box front over box back, matching bottom edges and leaving upper rim of box front free for opening.

Jack: Using patterns, cut one of each doll piece from color shown. Embroider face as follows, using two strands of floss in needle: two blue French-knot eyes; three black straight-stitch eyelashes above each eye; smiling mouth in red straight stitch (see Stitch Details, page 105). Assemble Jack as follows, using matching thread: Slip-stitch hair to top of head, leaving side "curls" free. Stitch bottom edge of face to body front at neck edge. Stitch rickrack across body front as shown in photograph. Pin body front to body back with edges even and straight edges of hands sandwiched between arms; whipstitch all around, leaving top of head open. Pin hat front to head back with edges even and "pompon" sandwiched between tips; stitch all around, leaving bottom edge of hat open. Stuff Jack through opening with fiberfill, using knitting needle to reach into arms and legs. Slip-stitch bottom of hat over top of hair. Cut 5" length from prepared bias tape. With matching thread, baste a line lengthwise along center fold of tape; pull to gather to 2½", forming "ruffle." Place ruffle around neck with basting thread at top and short raw edges meeting at back; stitch edges to back. Slip-stitch one half of Velcro® tab to center back of Jack; stitch opposite half to free end of tape extending from box. Bind bib edges with remaining bias tape, binding neck edges and making ties as for Noël Bib.

Santa and Elf

A cute twosome that can be made in no time at all—just work rounds of single crochet.

Santa and Elf

SIZE: 14″ high.

MATERIALS: Knitting worsted, 3 ounces red, 2 ounces pink, 1 ounce white, few yards of black, for Santa; 3 ounces green, 2 ounces red, 2 ounces pink, few yards of black and yellow for elf. Crochet hook size F. Stuffing. Scraps of black, red, yellow, and blue felt.

GAUGE: 4 sc = 1″. (To test gauge, see page 108.)

SANTA: With red, beg at top, ch 2.

Rnd 1: 6 sc in 2nd ch from hook. Mark end of rnds.

Rnd 2: 2 sc in each sc around.

Rnds 3 and 4: Work even on 12 sc.

Rnd 5: (Sc in next sc, 2 sc in next sc) 6 times.

Rnd 6: Work even on 18 sc.

Rnd 7: (Sc in next 2 sc, 2 sc in next sc) 6 times.

Rnd 8: Work even on 24 sc.

Rnd 9: (Sc in next 3 sc, 2 sc in next sc) 6 times.

Rnd 10: Work even on 30 sc.

Rnd 11: (Sc in next 4 sc, 2 sc in next sc) 6 times.

Rnd 12: Work even on 36 sc. Change to pink.

Rnds 13-21: Continue to inc 6 sc evenly around every other rnd 3 times more. Work 4 rnds even on 54 sc. Change to red.

Rnd 22-27: Work 6 rnds even. Change to black.

Rnd 28 and 29: Work 2 rnds even. Change to red.

Rnds 30 and 31: Work 2 rnds even.

Rnds 32-38: Dec 6 sc evenly around each rnd until 12 sc remain. (To dec 1 sc, pull up a lp in each of 2 sts, yo hook and through 3 lps on hook.) Before opening is too small, stuff body firmly. Gather remaining sts tog; sew opening closed.

Arms (make 2): With pink, ch 2.

Rnd 1: 6 sc in 2nd ch from hook.

Rnd 2: 2 sc in each sc around.

Rnd 3: (Sc in 3 sc, 2 sc in next sc) 3 times.

Rnds 4-6: Work even on 15 sc. Change to white.

Rnds 7 and 8: Work even. Change to red.

Rnds 9-17: Work even. End off. Stuff arms. Flatten top edge; sew opening closed; sew arms to sides above belt.

Legs (make 2): With black, ch 2.

Rnd 1: 6 sc in 2nd ch from hook.

Rnd 2: 2 sc in each sc around.

Rnd 3: (Sc in next sc, 2 sc in next sc) 6 times.

Rnds 4-6: Work even on 18 sc. Change to red.

Rnds 7-22: Work even. End off. Stuff legs. Flatten top edge; sew opening closed; sew legs to body.

FINISHING: Make a 1″ white pompon; sew to top of hat. With white, work 1 row of sc around lower edge of hat. For beard, thread double strand of white in yarn needle, work 2 rows of knotted loop st down each side and across lower edge of face. For mustache, wind yarn 30 times around 2 fingers. Tie tog at center, sew to face. From felt, cut 2 blue crescent eyes, red circular nose, yellow rectangular belt buckle. Glue in place.

ELF: With green, work as for Santa through rnd 12. Do not change to pink.

Rnd 13: (Sc in next 5 sc, 2 sc in next sc) 6 times.

Rnd 14: Work even on 42 sc.

Rnd 15: (Sc in next 6 sc, 2 sc in next sc) 6 times. Change to pink.

Rnds 16 and 17: Work even on 48 sc.

Rnds 18-23: Inc 6 sc evenly around on rnd 18. Work 5 rnds even on 54 sc. Change to red.

Rnds 24-29: Work 6 rnds even. Change to black.

Rnds 30 and 31: Work 2 rnds even. Change to green.

Rnds 32 and 33: Work 2 rnds even.

Rnds 34-40: Work and finish as for rnds 32–38 of Santa.

Arms: Work as for Santa, working rnds 1–6 in pink, 7–17 in green.

Legs: Work as for Santa, using green throughout.

Shoes (make 2): With green, ch 2.

Rnd 1: 6 sc in 2nd ch from hook.

Rnds 2 and 3: Work even.

Rnd 4: 2 sc in each sc around.

Rnds 5-8: Work even on 12 sc. End off. Stuff shoes lightly. Sew to bottom front of legs.

FINISHING: Make a 1″ red pompon; sew to top of hat. With red, work 1 row of sc around lower edge of hat. For hair, cut 15 2″ strands of yellow; tie tog at center; sew to center front under hat. From felt, cut 2 black crescent eyes, red circular nose and crescent mouth, yellow rectangular belt buckle. Glue in place.

Traveling Bears

A folding facade and rooftop handles allow this adorable crocheted bear family to pack up and move in a moment's notice.

Teddy Bear House and Furnishings

SIZE: 10″ high.

EQUIPMENT: Pencil. Ruler. Paper for patterns. Tailor's chalk. Scissors. Zigzag sewing machine.

MATERIALS:

For House: Closely woven cotton fabric, 45″ wide: candy stripe, ⅝ yard; holly print and solid green, ¼ yard each; white-and-green dotted, ⅜ yard; large scrap white for ceiling and appliqués; small scraps brown and red for appliqués. Scrap of black felt. Sewing thread to match fabrics. White eyelet lace, ¾″ wide, ⅝ yard. Scraps of white eyelet lace, 2¾″ wide, and val lace, ⅝″ wide. Polyester quilt batting. Large sheet of heavyweight cardboard. Sewing and embroidery needles. Six-strand embroidery floss, yellow and green.

For Furnishings: Scraps of cotton fabrics in assorted colors and prints (see color photograph). Large household sponge. Green, yellow, and red felt. Polyester fiberfill. Scraps of white braid trim. Lightweight cardboard. White glue. Sewing thread to match fabrics.

DIRECTIONS: Using pencil and ruler, draw lines across patterns, connecting grid lines. Enlarge patterns by copying on paper ruled in 1″ squares (see Enlarging the Pattern, page 103); complete half patterns, indicated by dash lines. Using patterns, cut pieces as directed below. Cut additional pieces without patterns as directed; seam allowance is included in measurements given. Except where otherwise indicated, stitch pieces together with right sides facing, making ½″ seams.

HOUSE:

Outside Walls and Base: From candy-striped fabric, cut 20¼″ × 13¼″ piece with stripes running vertically. Place on flat surface with right side up. Using tailor's chalk and a ruler, draw two parallel lines across piece, 6½″ and 13¾″ from one short (top) edge, dividing it into three rectangles. Read Appliqué, page 103. Using pattern, cut door from red fabric and machine-appliqué to top

rectangle (front wall), using matching thread, so that bottom edge of door is even with top marked line. Cut doorknob from black felt and glue to door where indicated on pattern. To make windows, cut two 3¼″ × 4″ pieces from white fabric and two 3¼″ pieces from 2½″-wide eyelet. Place eyelet on white pieces so that top 3¼″ edges are even; baste in place. Using pencil, lightly draw flowers along bottom edge of windows, following pattern and color illustration. Using two strands of floss in needle, embroider flowers as shown, using lazy daisy, straight stitches, and French knots (see Stitch Details, page 105). Machine-appliqué windows to wall on either side of door as shown, following appliqué directions and catching in edges of lace. From green fabric, cut two 1¾″ × 3½″ strips for window boxes. Fold each strip in half lengthwise and pin, folded edge up, below window, overlapping bottom of flower stems. Appliqué boxes to front wall along sides and bottom only. Pin 13¼″ piece of ¾″-wide eyelet along top edge of front wall as shown; baste. For roof, cut two 6½″ × 13¼″ pieces from green fabric. Pin pieces to top and bottom of striped piece; stitch, to make one 31¼″ × 13¼″ piece; press seams open. Using pattern, cut two side walls from candy-striped fabric, adding ½″ seams all around. Pin bottom of side walls to sides of middle section (base) and stitch, to form a single, cross-shaped piece; press seams open; set piece aside.

Inside Walls, Lawn, and Ceiling: Cut the following from fabric: one 6½″ × 13¼″ piece each from green (lawn) and white (ceiling); one 7″ × 13¼″ piece from holly print (back wall); one 13¼″ × 14¼″ piece from green dotted fabric (floor). Using pattern, cut mailbox from red fabric; cut ⅞″ × 3¼″ piece from white for post and 2″-3″ strip of brown to resemble walk (see color photograph). Appliqué walk and mailbox to lawn in positions shown. From white fabric, cut 3″ × 3½″ piece for window. Embroider flowers along bottom edge of window as for outside windows. Cut ⅝″-wide lace to fit sides and top of window for curtains; stitch in place. Appliqué window to back wall as shown. Pin ceiling, back wall, floor, and lawn to each other and stitch, making one 31¼″ × 13¼″ piece; press seams open. Using tailor's chalk, draw a horizontal line 12″ from bottom edge across floor, dividing it in two. Using pattern, cut two side walls from holly print fabric, adding ½″ all around for seam allowance. Pin bottom of side walls to sides of top section of floor (middle section of piece); stitch, to form a single, cross-shaped piece.

To Make House: To wrong side of each cross-shaped piece, baste one same-size piece of batting. Place pieces together, right sides facing and with edges even, and stitch sides together through all thicknesses, leaving top and bottom ends open; turn. Using pattern, cut two side walls from heavy cardboard and insert between layers of batting into piece. Cut 7¼″ × 12¼″ piece and insert into middle section (floor) between marked lines; cut two 6″ × 12¼″ pieces and insert into front and back walls; cut two 5½″ × 12¼″ pieces and insert into roof sections. Hand- or machine-baste between cardboard pieces through all thicknesses. From red fabric, cut two 2″ × 6″ strips for handles, double-fold, and stitch long sides, close to the edge. Turn ends of house ½″ to inside; pin handles in position shown and slip-stitch openings closed, catching in ends of handles between thicknesses. Fold side and back walls into upright position. Slip-stitch walls and roof together to form back of house as shown. Bring handles together to close front of house.

FURNISHINGS: Cut 4″ × 5″ × 1½″ piece of sponge for bed. From patchwork fabric (see color photograph), cut 7½″ × 8½″ piece for bedspread. Finish edges by folding ¼″ to wrong side and stitching. Place bedspread on bed and fold edges down around sides; make hospital corners. Slip-stitch edges of bedspread to bed all around. From remaining sponge piece, cut 1½″ × 4″ and 1½″ × 2″ pieces for sofa and chair seats. For backs, cut 3½″ × 4″ and 4″ × 2″ pieces from lightweight cardboard. To one side of each seat and back, glue a small piece of fiberfill for padding. Cover seats and padded side of backs with fabric cut to fit, gluing edges to bottom and to back. Cut piece to cover backs; glue. Glue backs to seats to make sofa and chair. Cut 2″

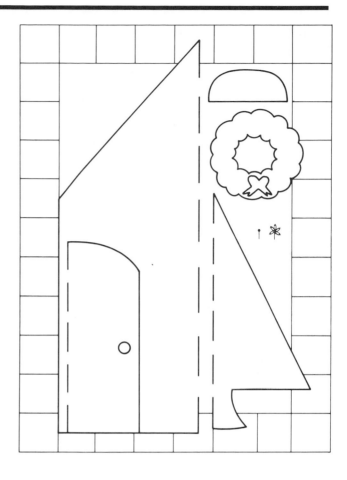

× 15″ and 2″ × 12″ fabric strips for "skirts"; turn edges of long sides ¼″ to wrong side and stitch. Starting and finishing in back, glue top edge of skirts to seats, making pleats along each side as you go. Cut trim and glue to sofa and chair as shown. To make pillows, cut two 1½″ fabric squares for each; glue edges together, with wrong sides facing, edges even, and small piece of fiberfill between. Using pattern, cut two tree pieces from print fabric, adding ¼″ seam allowance all around. With right sides facing, stitch pieces together, making ¼″ seams and leaving 1″ opening for turning; turn, stuff with fiberfill. Turn edges at opening ¼″ to inside and slip-stitch opening closed. To make table, cut one 2½″- and two 4″-diameter circles from yellow felt; cut 4″ circle from lightweight cardboard. Glue large circles together, with edges even and cardboard between. Cut 2½″ × 8½″ strip yellow felt and stitch one long side of strip to edge of small circle, making ¼″ seam and overlapping short ends of strip where they meet. Turn piece to form pedestal; slip-stitch along pedestal seam; stuff with fiberfill. Center large circle over open end of pedestal and slip-stitch pieces together to make table. Using pattern, cut one wreath from green felt and a bow from red felt; do not add seam allowance. Glue bow to wreath as shown; place wreath on door.

Teddy Bear Family

SIZE: Papa and Mama, 5″ high; twins, 4″ high.

MATERIALS: Mohair-type yarn, 1 50-gram ball each of tan and cream (to make all four bears). Crochet hook size D/3 (3¼ mm). Yarn needle. Stuffing. 8 small black shank-type buttons for eyes. Small amounts tan, black, and pink six-strand embroidery floss for mouth and nose.

Note: For extra fuzziness, each piece may be turned wrong-side out before stuffing.

PAPA AND MAMA: HEAD: Beg at tip of nose with cream, ch 2.

Rnd 1: 6 sc in 2nd ch from hook. Mark beg of each rnd for easier counting.

Rnd 2: (Sc in next sc, 2 sc in next sc) 3 times.

Rnd 3: Work even on 9 sc.

Rnd 4: (2 sc in next sc, sc in 2 sc) 3 times.

Rnd 5: Work even on 12 sc. Cut cream; attach tan.

Rnd 6: 2 sc in each of next 8 sc, sc in 4 sc—20 sc.

Rnd 7: Sc in 6 sc, 2 sc in each of 4 sc, sc in 10 sc—24 sc. Work 2 rnds even.

Rnd 10: (Sc in 5 sc, 2 sc in next sc) 4 times. Work 1 rnd even—28 sc.

Rnd 12: (Sc in 6 sc, sk 1 sc) 4 times. Work 1 rnd even—24 sc.

Rnd 14: (Sc in 5 sc, sk 1 sc) 4 times—20 sc.

Rnd 15: (Sc in 4 sc, sk 1 sc) 4 times—16 sc. Stuff head.

Rnd 16: (Sc in 3 sc, sk 1 sc) 4 times—12 sc.

Rnd 17: (Sc in next sc, sk 1 sc) 6 times; end off, leave end for sewing. Draw up stitches to close.

EARS: Work on rnd 10 of head, beg 6 sts to right of center top with tan, work sc in 4 sc, ch 1, turn. Sc in 4 sc, ch 1, turn. (Sc 2 sts tog) twice. Ch 1, turn. Sl st in 2nd st. End off. Sk 4 sc from first ear, make 2nd ear the same. Weave in yarn ends.

BODY: Beg at neck with tan, ch 10. Sl st in first ch to form ring.

Rnd 1: 12 sc in ring.

Rnd 2: (Sc in 2 sc, 2 sc in next sc) 4 times—16 sc.

Rnd 3: (Sc in next 3 sc, 2 sc in next sc) 4 times—20 sc. Work 1 rnd even.

Rnd 5: (Sc in 4 sc, 2 sc in next sc) 4 times. Work 4 rnds even—24 sc.

Divide for Legs: Rnd 1: Sc in 12 sc, ch 3, sk 12 sc.

Rnd 2: Sc in 12 sc, sc in each of 3 ch—15 sc.

Rnd 3: (Sc in 4 sc, sk next sc) 3 times—12 sc. Work next 4 rnds even.

Rnd 8: (Sc in next sc, sk next sc) 4 times, 2 sc in each of next 4 sc. Work 2 rnds even on 12 sc.

Rnd 11: (Sk next sc, sc in next sc) 6 times. End off, leave end for sewing. Draw up stitches to close. Sc around remaining leg opening, working 12 sc of body and 3 sc on opposite side of the ch 3. Complete as for first leg. Stuff legs and body. Sew head to body.

ARMS (make 2 for each bear): With tan, ch 2.

Rnd 1: 5 sc in 2nd ch from hook.

Rnd 2: 2 sc in each sc around—10 sc. Work next 6 rnds even. Sl st in next sc. End off, leave end for sewing. Stuff arms and sew to body at sides.

BEAR TWINS: HEAD: Beg at tip of nose with cream, ch 2.

Rnd 1: 6 sc in 2nd ch from hook. Mark beg of each rnd.

Rnd 2: (Sc in next sc, 2 sc in next sc) 3 times—9 sc.

Rnd 3: (2 sc in next sc, sc in 2 sc) 3 times—12 sc. Cut cream, attach tan.

Rnd 4: 2 sc in each of 8 sc, sc in 4 sc—20 sc.

Rnd 5: Sc in 6 sc, 2 sc in each of 4 sc, sc in 10 sc—24 sc. Work 2 rnds even.

Rnd 8: (Sc in 5 sc, sk 1 sc) 4 times—20 sc.

Rnd 9: (Sc in 4 sc, sk 1 sc) 4 times—16 sc.

Rnd 10: (Sc in 3 sc, sk 1 sc) 4 times—12 sc. Stuff head.

Rnd 11: (Sc in next sc, sk 1 sc) 6 times. End off; leave end for sewing. Draw up sts to close.

EARS: Working on rnd 7, beg 4 sts to right of center top, with tan, work sc in 3 sc; ch 1, turn. Sc in 3 sc, ch 1, turn. Sc next 2 sc tog; sl st in last sc. End off. Sk 2 sc from first ear, make 2nd ear the same. Weave in ends.

BODY: Beg at neck with tan, ch 8. Sl st in first ch to form ring.

Rnd 1: 10 sc in ring.

Rnd 2: (2 sc in next sc, sc in next sc) 5 times—15 sc.

Rnd 3: (2 sc in next sc, sc in next 2 sc) 5 times—20 sc. Work 2 rnds even.

Divide for Legs: Rnd 1: Sc in 10 sc, ch 2, sk next 10 sc.

Rnd 2: Sc in 10 sc, sc in each of 2 ch—12 sc.

Rnd 3: (Sc in 5 sc, sk 1 sc) twice—10 sc. Work 4 rnds even.

Rnd 8: (Sc in next sc, sk 1 sc) 5 times. End off, leave end for sewing. Draw up sts to close. Sc around remaining leg opening, working 10 sc of body and 2 sc on opposite side of ch 2. Complete as for first leg. Stuff legs and body. Sew head to body.

ARMS: (make 2 for each bear): With tan, ch 2.

Rnd 1: 4 sc in 2nd ch from hook.

Rnd 2: 2 sc in each sc around—8 sc. Work 5 rnds even. Sl st in next sc. End off, leaving

yarn end for sewing. Stuff arms and sew to body at sides.

FINISHING: Sew button eyes to face.

Embroidery (use 3 strands embroidery floss): With tan, embroider nose in satin stitch. With black, embroider mouth in outline stitch. Embroider Mama Bear's mouth with pink satin stitch and eyelashes with several straight stitches (see Stitch Details, page 105).

Teddy Bear Clothes

SIZE: To fit crocheted bears.

EQUIPMENT: Pencil. Ruler. Paper for pattern. Scissors.

MATERIALS: Scraps of cotton fabrics in red, red stripe, and green. Pre-gathered cotton print ruffle, 1½" wide, ⅜ yard. Red double-fold bias tape, ¼" wide. Sewing thread to match fabrics.

DIRECTIONS: Using pencil and ruler, draw lines across patterns, connecting grid lines. Enlarge patterns by copying on paper ruled in

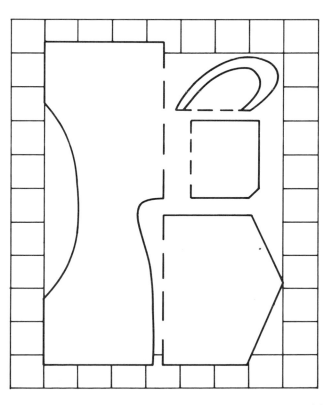

½" squares (see Enlarging the Pattern, page 103); complete half patterns, indicated by dash lines. Use patterns to cut out pieces as directed, adding ³⁄₁₆" seam allowance all around.

VEST: Using pattern, cut one vest each from red and red-striped fabric. Place pieces together with right sides facing and edges even and stitch ³⁄₁₆" seam all around, leaving 1" opening for turning. Clip corners and curves and turn vest right side out; press. Turn raw edges at opening to inside and slip-stitch closed. Place vest on Papa bear.

TROUSERS AND SHORTS: Using pattern, cut two pieces each for shorts and trousers from green fabric. Turn seam allowance along top and bottom edges (see pattern) to wrong side and stitch. Place matching pieces together with right sides facing and edges even, and, beginning at dot, stitch A sides together with ³⁄₁₆" seam; end ¼" from top on one side only to make opening. Open piece into a tube and refold so that B sides are even

and seams match at center; stitch B sides together, making ³⁄₁₆" seam. Turn trousers right side out and place on Papa bear with opening at back; tack top of opening closed. For shorts, make bib following directions below and slip-stitch to waist front as shown. Place on Boy bear and stitch opening as for trousers.

PINAFORES: Using patterns, cut two large and two small bibs from red fabric, adding ³⁄₁₆" seam allowance all around. Place matching pieces together, right sides facing and edges even, and stitch around; leave a 1" opening at bottom for turning. Clip curves, turn, and press. Turn raw edges to inside and slip-stitch closed. From ruffle, cut 4½" piece (Girl) and 5½" piece (Mama) for pinafore skirts. Enclose top edge of each with bias tape cut to fit and slip-stitch. Fold each skirt in half widthwise, with right side in, and stitch ³⁄₁₆" seam to within ¼" of bias tape, leaving skirt opening. Turn skirt to right side. Slip-stitch bib to waist front as shown. Place pinafores on Mama and Girl bears; tack tops of skirt openings closed.

Great Gifts

Crochet a sporty novelty stocking. Make a child's doggy bag tote (with its own tiny felt pooch), a roomy Santa tote, or cuddly baby sister, sewn, stuffed, and dressed in frills.

Novelty Stockings

SIZE: Each stocking measures about 16″ high.

GAUGE: 11 sc = 3″ (To test gauge, see page 108.)

GENERAL NOTES: Cut and join colors as needed.

To Dec 1 St: Pull a lp in each of 2 sts, yo hook and through 3 lps on hook.

To Inc 1 St: Work 2 sts in same st.

RED SHOE: MATERIALS: Worsted weight yarns: 2 ounces red (A); 1 ounce each of black (B), Nile green (C), bright pink (D), lime green (E), amethyst (F), dark green (G), pink (H), dark turquoise (I), and lilac (J). Crochet hook size H. Yarn needle.

Sole: With B, ch 24.

Rnd 1: Sc in 2nd ch from hook and in each of next 14 ch, hdc in each of next 3 ch, dc in each of next 4 ch, 5 dc in last ch (front); working on other side of starting ch, dc in each of next 4 ch, hdc in each of next 3 ch, sc in each of next 15 ch, 3 sc in turning ch (back). Mark for end of rnd. Do not join or turn.

Rnd 2: Sc around, work 2 sc in each of front 5 sc and 2 sc in each of back 3 sc—60 sc.

Rnd 3: Sc around, inc 4 sts across front and back—68 sc.

Rnds 4 and 5: Repeat rnd 3—84 sc.

Rnd 6: Sc in each sc around. Sl st in next sc; end off.

Foot: Join A at center back of sole. From right side, working in back lp, sc in each sc around. Join with a sl st in first sc. Ch 1, turn each rnd.

Rnds 2-9: Sc in each sc. Join. End off at end of last rnd.

Shape Top: From wrong side, join A in 28th st from center back; ch 1, sc in each sc to center back and in each of next 28 sc—56 sc. Ch 1, turn. Work back and forth on these 56 sts for 4 rows. Ch 1, turn.

Next Row: Sc in each of next 10 sts. Ch 1, turn.

Next Row: Dec 1 sc each side—8 sc.

Next Row: Sc in each sc—8 sc.

Next Row (eyelet row): Dec 1 sc, sc in next sc, ch 2, sk next 2 sc, sc in next sc, dec 1 sc. Ch 1, turn.

Next Row: Sc in each st and ch across—6 sc. End off. Work other side to correspond.

Tongue: Beg at front edge, with A, ch 7.

Row 1: Sc in 2nd ch from hook and in each ch across—6 sc. Ch 1, turn each row.

Rows 2-4: Inc 1 st each side—12 sc. Work even in sc for 20 rows. Dec 1 st each side every row 4 times—4 sts. End off.

Stocking: Beg at lower edge, with C, ch 50. Being careful not to twist ch, sl st in first ch, forming ring.

Rnd 1: Ch 3 (counts as 1 dc), dc in each ch around—50 dc. Join with a sl st in top of ch 3; turn each rnd.

Rnd 2: With D, ch 3, dc in each dc around. Repeating rnd 2, work 1 rnd each of E, F, H, I, A, G, H, B, C, F, I, E, B, A, J, D, G, I, A, C, F, H, B. At end of last rnd, ch 10 for loop, sl st in next st. End off.

FINISHING: Sew tongue to front of shoe. With B, work 1 rnd sc around upper edge of shoe and tongue. With B, work buttonhole st around eyelets. Sew stocking to inside of shoe and tongue.

Tie: With H, ch 100. Sc in each ch. End off. Pull tie through eyelets; tie into bow.

ANKLE-HIGH SNEAKER: MATERIALS: Worsted weight yarns: 2 ounces red (A); 1 ounce each of white (B), blue (C), and pink (D). Crochet hook size H. Yarn needle.

Sole: With B, work same as for Red Shoe.

Foot: Join B at center back of sole. From right side, working in back lp, sc in each sc around. Join with a sl st in first sc; do not turn.

Rnd 2: Ch 1, sc in each sc around. Join; do

not turn. Repeating rnd 2, work 1 rnd A, 2 rnds B. End off.

Shape Top: From right side, join C in 28th st from center back, ch 1, sc in each st to center back and in each of next 28 sts—56 sc. Ch 1, turn each row.

Rows 2-4: Dec 1 sc each side—50 sc.

Row 5 (eyelet row): Dec 1 sc, sc in next sc, ch 1, sk next sc, sc in each sc to within last 4 sts, ch 1, sk next sc, sc in next sc, dec 1 st.

Row 6: Sc in each st across, dec 1 st each side—46 sc.

Row 7: Dec 2 sc, sc in next sc, ch 1, sk next sc, sc in each sc to within last 6 sts, ch 1, sk next sc, sc in next sc, dec 2 sc.

Row 8: Dec 2 sc each side.

Row 9: Repeat row 5.

Rows 10-13: Sc in each st across—36 sc.

Row 14: Sc in each of first 2 sc, ch 1, sk next sc, sc in each sc to within last 3 sc, end ch 1, sk next sc, sc in each of last 2 sc.

Rows 15-18: Sc in each sc across—36 sc.

Rows 19 and 20: Repeat rows 14 and 15.

Rows 21 and 22: Dec 1 st each side—32 sts. End off.

Tongue: Beg at lower edge, with B, work rows 1–13 same as for Red Shoe—12 sc.

Row 14: With C, sc in back lp of each st across. Work in sc for 29 rows.

Rows 44-46: Dec 1 st each side—6 sts.

Row 47: (Pull up a lp in each of next 3 sts, yo hook and through 4 lps on hook) twice. End off.

Circles (make 2): With B, ch 4; join with a sl st in first ch, forming ring.

Rnd 1: Ch 1, 8 sc in ring. Join with a sl st in first sc; do not turn.

Rnd 2: 2 sc in each sc. Join; end off.

Stocking: Beg at lower edge, with A, ch 45. Being careful not to twist ch, sl st in first ch, forming ring.

Rnd 1: Ch 3 (counts as 1 dc), dc in each ch around—45 dc. Join with a sl st in top of ch 3; turn each rnd.

Rnd 2: Ch 3, dc in each dc around. Repeating rnd 2, work 2 rnds D, 2 rnds A alternately until 22 rnds from start. At end of last rnd, ch 10 for loop, sl st in next st. End off.

Shoe Lace: With A, ch 200. Sc in 2nd ch from hook and in each ch across. End off.

FINISHING: Sew tongue to front of sneaker, tack upper edge of sneaker to tongue. From right side, with B, work 1 rnd sc around edge of sneaker; with C, work sc across upper edge of tongue. With B, work buttonhole st around eyelets. Sew circles in place. Sew stocking to inside of sneaker and tongue. With shoe lace, lace up front of sneaker.

MARY JANE: MATERIALS: Worsted weight yarns, 4 ounces white (A), 1 ounce each of black (B) and lilac (C). Crochet hook size H. One button. Yarn needle. Stuffing.

Sole: With B, work same as for Red Shoe.

Foot: Join C at center back of sole. From right side, working in back lp, sc in each sc around. Join with a sl st in first sc.

Next Rnd: Ch 1, sc in each sc around. Join; end off.

Beg at front edge of top of foot, with C, ch 9.

Row 1: Sc in 2nd ch from hook and in each ch across—8 sc. Ch 1, turn.

Row 2: Inc 1 st each side—10 sc. Ch 1, turn each row.

Rows 3-6: Repeat row 2—18 sc.

Rows 7-15: Sc in each st across.

Row 16: Sc in each of next 5 sts, dec 1 sc. Ch 1, turn.

Row 17: Sc in each sc—6 sc. Ch 1, turn.

Rows 18-22: Repeat row 17.

Row 23: Sc in each sc across, ch 14 for strap. Turn.

Row 24: Sc in 5th ch from hook and in each ch and st across.

Row 25: Sc in 6 sc. Ch 1, turn.

Rows 26-42: Sc in each sc. End off. Sk 4 sc on last long row; with C, dec 1 st, sc in each remaining 5 sc. Ch 1, turn. Work in sc for 26 rows. End off.

Heel: With B, ch 7.

Row 1: Sc in 2nd ch from hook, sc in each of next 4 ch, 3 sc in last ch; working on other side of starting ch, sc in each of next 5 ch—13 sc. Ch 1, turn.

Row 2: Sc in each of next 5 sc, 2 sc in each of next 3 sc, sc in each of next 5 sc—16 sc. Ch 1, turn each row.

Row 3: Sc in each of next 6 sc, 2 sc in each of next 4 sc, sc in each of next 6 sc—20 sc.

Row 4: Sc in each of next 6 sc, 2 sc in next sc, sc in next sc, 2 sc in next sc, sc in each of next 2 sc, 2 sc in next sc, sc in next sc, 2 sc in next sc, sc in each of next 6 sc—24 sc.

Row 5: Sc in each of next 7 sc, 2 sc in next sc, sc in next sc, 2 sc in next sc, sc in each of next 4 sc, 2 sc in next sc, sc in next sc, 2 sc in next sc, sc in each of next 7 sc—28 sc.

Row 6: Sc in each sc.

Row 7: Working in back lp, sc in each sc; do not turn; continue to work 14 sc across straight edge of heel. Join with a sl st in first sc; do not turn.

Rnds 9-14: Sc in each sc around—42 sc. Join with a sl st in first sc. End off.

Stocking: Beg at lower edge, with A, ch 45. Join with a sl st in first ch, forming ring.

Rnd 1: Sc in each ch around. Do not join. Work around in sc until piece measures 12¾" from start.

Next Rnd: Sc in next sc, ch 3, sl st in 3rd ch from hook (picot made), sk next sc, repeat from * around, end ch 10 for lp, sl st in next sc. End off.

Front Stocking: Join A in 19th st from center of back on lower edge of stocking, sc in each of next 9 sc. Ch 1, turn. Work in sc on these 9 sts for 8 rows. End off.

FINISHING: Sew back seam on foot; weave upper foot to lower foot. From right side, with B, work 1 rnd sc around upper edge of foot and strap. Sew on button. Stuff heel firmly; sew to back of sole. Sew stocking to inner edge of shoe as pictured.

SPORT SHOE: MATERIALS: Worsted weight yarns, 2 ounces white (A); 4 ounces red (B); 1 ounce each of black (C) and dark gold (D). Crochet hook size H.

Sole: With A, work same as for Red Shoe.

Foot: Join A at center back of sole. From right side, working in back lp, sc in each sc around. Join with a sl st in first sc.

Rnd 2: Ch 1, sc in each sc around. Join; end off.

Beg at front edge of top of foot, with C, ch 9.

Row 1: Sc in 2nd ch from hook and in each ch across—8 sc. Ch 1, turn each row.

Row 2: Inc 1 sc each side—10 sc.

Rows 3-6: Repeat row 2—18 sc.

Rows 7-17: Working in sc, work 5 rows C, 2 rows A, 2 rows C, 2 rows A.

Row 18: With C, sc in each of next 9 sc. Ch 1, turn.

Rows 19-22: Working on these 9 sc, work 4 rows.

Row 23: Dec 1 sc, sc in each sc—8 sc.

Row 24: Sc in each sc.

Rows 25 and 26: Repeat rows 23 and 24.

Row 27: Repeat row 23—6 sc. Work 13 rows even. End off. Join C in next sc on last long row; work to correspond to other side. Weave back seam.

Back Heel Piece: With A, ch 5.

Row 1: Sc in 2nd ch from hook and in each ch across—4 sc. Ch 1, turn each row. Inc 1 st each side of next row, then every other row twice more—10 sc. Work 1 row even. End off.

Tongue: Beg at front edge with C, ch 5.

Row 1: Sc in 2nd ch from hook and in each ch across—4 sc. Ch 1, turn each row.

Row 2: Inc 1 st each side—6 sc.

Row 3 (eyelet row): Inc 1 st, ch 1, sk next st, sc in each of next 2 sc, ch 1, sk next st, inc 1 st in last st.

Row 4: Sc in each st across—8 sc.

Row 5: Repeat row 2—10 sc.

Row 6: Sc in each of next 2 sts, ch 1, sk next st, sc in each of next 4 sts, ch 1, sk next st, sc in each of last 2 sts. Work 2 rows even.

Row 9: Repeat row 6. Work 2 rows even.

Row 12: Repeat row 6. Work 2 rows even. Dec 1 st each side of next 2 rows. End off.

Shoe Lace: With D, ch 150. Sc in 2nd ch from hook and in each ch across. End off.

Spikes (make 8): With A, ch 4, sl st in first ch, forming ring.

Rnd 1: 6 sc in ring. Do not join.

Rnd 2: Sc in each sc. End off, leaving a 10″ end for sewing.

Stocking: With B, ch 51.

Row 1: Sc in 2nd ch from hook and in each ch across—50 sc. Ch 1, turn each row.

Row 2: Working in back lp, sc in each sc across.

Row 3: Working in both lps, sc in each sc across.

Rows 4-44: Repeat rows 2 and 3, end row 2. End off. Weave last row to starting ch for back seam.

Cuff: With B, work 1 rnd sc around upper edge of stocking; join with a sl st in first sc. Turn.

Rnd 2: Ch 3, dc in each st around. Join; turn.

Rnd 3: With A, ch 3, dc in each st around. Join; turn. Repeating rnd 3, work 1 rnd B, 1 rnd A, 1 rnd B. End off. Fold cuff to right side. With B, make 10 ch at back seam for lp.

FINISHING: Weave upper foot to top edge of lower foot. Weave lower edge of back heel

piece to back of foot. From right side, with A, work 1 rnd sc around upper edge of foot, catching in top edge of back heel piece. With A, work 1 row sc around side and lower edge of tongue. Sew tongue to foot as pictured. Sew spikes to bottom of sole. Lace up tongue with tie. Sew stocking to inner edge of foot.

Doggie and Santa Totes

SIZE: Doggie Tote, 8″ × 9¾″; Santa Tote, 16½″ × 17½″.

EQUIPMENT: Colored pencil. Pencil. Ruler. Paper for patterns. Scissors. Straight pins. Dressmaker's tracing (carbon) paper. Dry ball-point pen. Sewing needle. Sewing machine with zigzag stitch. Iron.

MATERIALS:

For Doggie Tote: Medium-weight cotton or cotton-blend fabric, 36″ wide: yellow calico, ¼ yard; red, ¼ yard. Heavy-weight interfacing, ⅓ yard. Felt scraps: tan, blue, red, orange, yellow. Blue ribbon, ¼″ wide, 9½″. Pompons ⅜″ diameter, two yellow, one orange. Matching thread. Fiberfill. Black marking pen. White glue.

For Santa Tote: Heavy-weight fabric such as duck, 45″ wide, red, ⅞ yard. Red/white striped fabric, two 10¼″ × 9″ pieces. Fabric scraps: green, pink, white for appliqués. Red, white, green, black thread. White pompon.

GENERAL DIRECTIONS: Using sharp colored pencil, draw lines across patterns, connecting grid lines. Enlarge patterns by copying on paper ruled in 1″ squares (see Enlarging the Pattern, page 103). Cut pattern pieces from designated fabrics, adding ¼″ seam allowance unless otherwise directed. Cut front, back, side, bottom, and strap pieces according to measurements in individual directions; seam allowance is included. Stitch all pieces together with right sides facing, making ¼″ seams.

Finish front and back pieces, including pocket, following individual directions. Pin and stitch each side piece to bottom at short

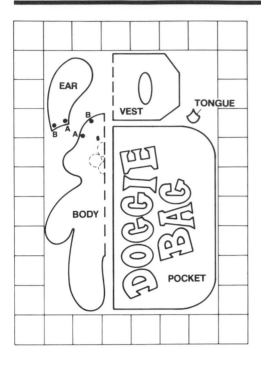

edges to make one long strip. Pin back piece to strip, matching bottom corners to seams. Stitch together, turning stitching or rounding at corners as desired. Pin and stitch front piece to strip in same manner. Trim top edges of bag evenly if necessary. Turn raw top edge ¼" to wrong side; stitch in place. Turn under again ¾"; stitch close to fold. Topstitch around bag close to each side and bottom seam. For straps, fold each strap piece in half lengthwise; stitch across long edge and one short edge. Turn to right side; turn raw edge ¼" to inside and press; topstitch closed. Attach straps to bag, following individual directions.

DOGGIE TOTE: Cut from yellow calico: two 9¼" × 10¼" pieces for front and back; one pocket strip, 6¾" × 1". From red fabric, cut one pocket from pattern, adding ¼" seam allowance; one strap, 35½" × 3½"; one front strip, 10¼" × 2"; two sides, 9½" × 3¼"; one bottom, 10¼" × 3¼". Cut one front, one back, two sides, one bottom, and one pocket from interfacing, using above measurements.

Stitch interfacing to wrong side of each piece close to raw edge, except for pocket.

To make pocket, pin a long edge of pocket strip to top edge of pocket; stitch together. Press strip upward; topstitch strip close to

seam. Stitch interfacing to pocket piece with right sides facing, leaving 2" opening for turning. Turn to right side; turn raw edges to inside and slip-stitch opening closed. Use patterns to cut letters from yellow felt (do not add seam allowance). Glue to front of pocket as shown. For front of bag, turn a long edge of front strip ¼" to wrong side and press. Pin strip to top edge of front, matching raw edges; stitch along raw edges; fold strip over to right side and topstitch pressed edge. Center pocket on front and topstitch in place around curved edges. Complete bag and make strap, following General Directions. Stitch strap ends securely to sides of bag.

To make dog, cut the following pieces from felt: two tan bodies and one blue vest, placing dash lines on fold of fabric and adding ¼" seam allowance; cut two orange ears and one red tongue, without allowance. Cut out each armhole on vest. Pin ears between dots on one body piece, matching A-B edges. Pin and stitch body pieces together with ears in between, leaving opening for turning. Turn to right side, exposing ears; stuff with fiberfill until firm. Turn raw edges at opening to inside; slip-stitch closed. Following fine dash lines on pattern, glue tongue in position, glue two yellow pompons over tongue for muzzle, and glue orange pompon in place for nose. Use marking pen to mark eyes. Place vest on dog, tie blue ribbon bow around neck; place dog into pocket on bag.

SANTA TOTE: Cut from red fabric: two 18" × 16¾" pieces for front and back; two straps, 3" × 45"; two sides, 6½" × 18¼"; one bottom, 18" × 6½".

For pocket, use dressmaker's carbon and dry ball-point pen to transfer outlines of Santa appliqué design to right side of one striped piece; omit fine lines, which indicate embroidery. Make a separate pattern for each appliqué; use patterns to cut pieces from fabric scraps, following illustration, and adding ⅛" seam allowance. Pin appliqués to pocket in marked positions; baste in place. Set sewing machine for close zigzag stitch; zigzag around appliqués, covering raw edges and ⅛" excess fabric. Remove basting. Transfer embroidery lines to face; zigzag-stitch along

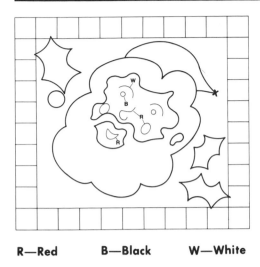

R—Red   B—Black   W—White

lines and fill in cheeks and eyes, following color key. Pin pocket pieces together with right sides facing; stitch around all edges, leaving opening for turning. Turn to right side; turn raw edges to inside and press. Slip-stitch opening closed. Sew pompon to end of Santa's hat at X.

For straps, measure and mark line 6½" in and parallel to each side (16¾") edge on front and back pieces. Make straps, following General Directions. Center one strap over marked lines on each piece with ends of strap even with bottom edges of bag; excess strap extending from top becomes handle. Stitch each long edge in place; end stitching 2" from top. Center pocket over straps on one piece; stitch in place. Assemble bag, following General Directions. After hemming top edge, finish stitching straps to top edge of bag.

Baby Sister

SIZE: About 18″ long.

EQUIPMENT: Colored pencil. Pencil. Ruler. Paper for patterns. Scissors. Tape measure. Straight pins. Dressmaker's tracing (carbon) paper. Dry ball-point pen. Sewing, embroidery needles. Sewing machine. Small embroidery hoop. Iron. Small safety pin.

MATERIALS: Closely woven cotton or cotton-blend fabric, 45″ wide, ½ yard pink; ½ yard baby green. White eyelet fabric with finished scalloped edge, 36″ wide, 1 yard.

White eyelet trim, ¼″ wide, ⅓ yard. White ruffled eyelet trim, ½″ wide, 2¾ yards. White satin ribbon, ¼″ wide, 1⅓ yards. White elastic, ⅛″ wide, 1 yard. Mohair-type yarn for hair, 4 ounces copper. White ¼″ button. Pink felt scrap. Matching thread. Six-strand embroidery floss: brown, light green, dark green, pale pink, pink, white. Polyester fiberfill. Glue.

DIRECTIONS: Using sharp colored pencil, draw lines across patterns below, connecting grid lines. Enlarge patterns by copying on paper ruled in 1″ squares (see Enlarging the Pattern, page 103); complete half-patterns, indicated by heavy dash lines. Fine lines indicate embroidery. Use patterns to mark the following pieces on wrong side of pink fabric, leaving ½″ between each and reversing patterns for second and fourth of duplicate pieces: two head sides, two body fronts, two body backs, four arms, and four legs; do not cut out. Mark one head on right side of fabric. Using dressmaker's carbon and dry ball-point pen, transfer face markings to right side of head. Place fabric in hoop, centering face. Using three strands of floss in needle, outline-stitch eyelashes and eye outlines in brown; satin-stitch eyes, making irises dark green and making pupils light green; highlight pupils and embroider tooth with white satin stitch. Using two strands of floss in needle, satin-stitch pale pink nose; outline-stitch mouth with pink; make two small straight stitches on each side. See Stitch Details, page 105.

Cut out all pieces, adding ¼″ seam allowance all around. With right sides facing, pin and sew pieces together as directed, making ¼″ seams. Clip into seam allowances at curves to ease.

To make body, stitch body fronts together along center seams; stitch body backs together. Stitch small button (belly button) to front at open circle on pattern. Stitch front to back, matching A's and crotch seams. Turn to right side and stuff with fiberfill until full. Stitch two pairs of arms and two pairs of legs together, leaving straight edges open; turn to right side; stuff until firm. Turn raw edges at openings ¼″ to inside; slip-stitch openings closed. Slip-stitch arms to body between B's; stitch legs to body between C's. Cut heart

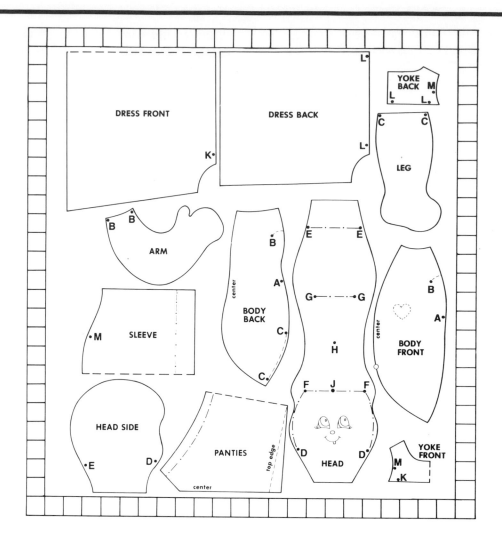

from pink felt, using dash lines on body front for pattern; glue in position. To make head, stitch head sides to head matching D and E; ease fabric at curves. Turn and stuff same as for body.

Make hair as follows: Thread embroidery needle with one strand of yarn. Insert needle at one F and work row of running stitches across dot/dash line to opposite F, making one 7″ loop with each stitch. Thread needle with more yarn as necessary. Repeat procedure on dot/dash line between G's, making 9″ loops. Brush all loops away from center of head, exposing crown. Leaving 4″ length of yarn free, tack yarn to head at one D; run yarn over crown behind 7″ loops; tack at opposite D; make 4″ loop, securing with small stitch; run yarn back across head, keeping lengths of yarn flush; make 4″ loop. Run yarn back and forth across head, making a loop at each end and covering crown between G and F lines.

Stitch yarn to head in any areas where it tends to move out of place. Grasp loops brushed over forehead and back of head; bring them together over top of head at H, arrange to make small bun and tie with yarn. Tie 12″ length of white satin ribbon in a bow around bun. Cover back of head same as crown, making 4″ loops all around and along dot/dash line between E's. Fold loops up to simulate a flip; slip-stitch in place. Wrap yarn around finger five times; remove from finger and slip-stitch loops to head at J. Place head over body; slip-stitch.

Clothes: To make dress, cut pieces from green fabric as follows: one yoke front, two yoke backs, two sleeves, one dress front, two dress backs. Stitch yoke backs to yoke front at shoulders. Turn neck edge ¼″ to wrong side and press, clipping fabric as necessary. Pin eyelet trim to wrong side of neck so ruffle extends beyond edge; stitch in place. Machine-baste across top edges of dress front and backs between dots K and L; pull basting thread to gather fabrics. Pin dress backs to yoke backs, and dress front to yoke front, adjusting gathers and matching dots. Stitch together; press seams toward yoke. For each sleeve, turn bottom edge ¼" to wrong side and press; stitch eyelet trim to edge same as for neck. Cut 4½" length of elastic; pin to sleeve over dot/dash line. Zigzag-stitch elastic in place, pulling elastic to fit as you stitch. Machine-baste around sleeve cap between M's; pull basting thread to gather fabric to fit armhole edge. Pin in place, adjusting gathers and matching M's; stitch. Stitch sides together from hem to end of sleeve trim, matching underarm seams. Make ¼" hem on dress; stitch eyelet trim to hem as for sleeves. Turn edges of dress back under twice; stitch in place. Cut two 7" lengths of white satin ribbon; stitch one to each side of yoke back at neck edge.

To make apron, cut 36" × 6" strip from eyelet fabric, with one long edge of strip placed on scalloped edge for hem. Turn all raw edges under twice; stitch in place.

Machine-baste across upper edge and gather fabric to 14" width. Cut 33" length of satin ribbon; mark center and mark 7" to left and right of center. Place ribbon over top edge of apron, matching side edges to markings; stitch in place, securing gathers. Cut eyelet trim into two 6" lengths for straps. Stitch one end of each strap to back edge of apron; try apron on doll, and pin other end of straps in position on apron front. Stitch in place.

To make panties, cut two pieces from eyelet fabric using pattern; cut away fabric on one piece along dash lines at top edge for front. Stitch pieces together at center edges to make a tube. Turn top edge under ⅛" and then ½" to make a casing; stitch in place, leaving opening for elastic. Cut 11" length of elastic; run through casing using safety pin. Stitch ends of elastic together; stitch opening closed. Turn raw edges of leg openings ¼" to wrong side; press. Stitch eyelet trim to each leg edge as for sleeves. Cut two 7" lengths of elastic; pin and stitch to dot/dash line on each leg same as for sleeve. With seams matching, pin and stitch crotch seam; turn to right side and place on baby.

Dolls, Dolls, Dolls

Sitting pretty are these favorite companions of every youngster: knitted snowman, crocheted Blondie, colorful disk doll, little Humpty-Dumpty, Blondie's twin brother Butch, Marty Mouse, and long-legged Pinafore Pattie.

Snowman

SIZE: 12″ tall.

MATERIALS: Acrylic cotton or rayon rug yarn, 3 ounces white, 1 ounce black, small amount red. Set of dp needles No. 10. Crochet hook size H. Four white buttons. Two black buttons for eyes. Orange chenille stick. Scrap of red felt.

GAUGE: 3 sts = 1″ (To test gauge, see page 111.)

SNOWMAN: BODY: Beg at lower edge, with white, cast on 20 sts. Divide sts on 3 needles. Join, k 2 rnds.

Rnd 3: Inc 4 sts evenly around. K 2 rnds even.

Rnd 6: Inc 4 sts evenly around. K 2 rnds even.

Rnd 9: Inc 4 sts evenly around. K 14 rnds even—32 sts.

Rnd 24: Dec 4 sts evenly. K 2 rnds even.

Rnd 27: Dec 4 sts evenly. K 2 rnds even.

Rnd 30: (K 2 tog) 12 times. K 1 rnd.

Rnd 32: Inc 1 st in each st. K 1 rnd—24 sts.

Rnd 34: Inc 4 sts evenly. K 1 rnd.

Rnd 36: Inc 4 sts evenly. K 8 rnds even—32 sts.

Rnd 43: Dec 4 sts evenly. K 1 rnd.

Rnd 45: Dec 4 sts evenly. K 1 rnd.

Rnd 47: Dec 4 sts evenly. Cut yarn; weave top of head tog with Kitchener st. (see detail).

LEG (make 2): Beg at lower edge, with white, cast on 20 sts. K 5 rnds.

Rnd 6: K 6, k 2 tog, k 4, sl 1, k 1, psso, k 6.

Rnd 7: K 5, k 2 tog, k 4, sl 1, k 1, psso, k 5. K 20 rnds on 16 sts.

Rnd 28: Dec 4 sts evenly around. K 1 rnd. Cut yarn, weave top of leg tog.

ARM (make 2): Beg at top edge, with white, cast on 14 sts. K 17 rnds.

Rnd 18: Inc 2 sts in rnd. K 5 rnds even.

Rnd 24: Dec 4 sts in rnd. K 1 rnd. Cut yarn; weave end of hand tog.

FINISHING: Stuff body, arms, and legs. Sew openings tog. Sew buttons on arms and legs through body so arms and legs will move. Sew on button eyes. Form a coil with chenille stick; sew one end to face for nose. Cut crescent mouth from red felt; sew or glue on. Make 3 black "buttons": ch 2; 6 sc in 2nd ch from hook. Sew to front of body.

SCARF: With red and 2 needles, cast on 4 sts. Knit each row until scarf is 16″ long. Fringe ends.

HAT: With black, ch 2.

Rnd 1: 6 sc in 2nd ch from hook.

Rnd 2: 2 sc in each sc around.

Rnd 3: (Sc in next sc, 2 sc in next sc) 6 times.

Rnds 4-7: Sc in each sc around—18 sc.

Rnd 8: (Sc in 2 sc, 2 sc in next sc) 6 times.

Rnd 9: (Sc in 3 sc, 2 sc in next sc) 6 times.

Rnd 10: (Sc in 4 sc, 2 sc in next sc) 6 times. Sl st in first sc of rnd. End off.

TO WEAVE WITH KITCHENER STITCH: Stitches are evenly divided on two needles and held parallel, with yarn coming from first stitch on back needle. Break off yarn, leaving about 12″ end on work. Thread this end into a tapestry needle. Working from right to left, * pass needle through first stitch on front needle as if to knit and slip stitch off needle, pass yarn through 2nd stitch on front needle as if to purl but leave stitch on needle, pass yarn through first stitch on back needle as if to purl and slip stitch off needle; pass yarn through 2nd stitch on back needle as if to knit, but leave on needle. Repeat from * until all stitches are woven. See illustration above.

Humpty Dumpty Rattle

SIZE: 6″ high.

MATERIALS: Worsted weight yarn, small amounts of white, red, blue, and yellow. Crochet hook size G. L'eggs® container. Pink, rose and red embroidery floss. Small amount of stuffing. Bell, pebbles, or beans for rattle. Glue.

GAUGE: 4 sc = 1″. (To test gauge, see page 108.)

HUMPTY DUMPTY: BODY: With white, ch 2.

Rnd 1: 6 sc in 2nd ch from hook.

Rnd 2: 2 sc in each sc around.

Rnd 3: (2 sc in next sc, sc in next sc) 6 times.

Rnd 4: (Sc in 5 sc, 2 sc in next sc) 3 times—21 sc.

Rnd 5: (Sc in 6 sc, 2 sc in next sc) 3 times—24 sc.

Rnd 6: (Sc in 7 sc, 2 sc in next sc) 3 times—27 sc.

Rnds 7-10: Continue to inc 3 sc each rnd—39 sc.

Rnds 11 and 12: Work even on 39 sc for 2 rnds. Sl st in next sc. End off.

Rnds 13-15: Join red with sc in sc before sl st, sc in each sc around for 3 rnds. Sl st in next sc. End off.

Rnd 16: Join blue, (sc in 11 sc, work next 2 sc tog) 3 times—36 sc.

Rnd 17: (Sc in 10 sc, work 2 sc tog) 3 times—33 sc.

Rnds 18-21: Continue to dec 3 sc each rnd, slipping plastic egg in pointed end first (containing rattle material and glued shut), after rnd 18.

Rnd 22: Work 2 sc tog around until 5 sc remain, sl st in next sc. End off; sew opening closed with yarn end.

ARMS (make 2): With red, ch 2; 6 sc in 2nd ch from hook. Work in sc, inc 3 sc in next rnd, then work even on 9 sc for 4 rnds. End off; leave end for sewing. Stuff arms, sew to red body on opposite sides, slightly toward front.

LEGS (make 2): With blue, ch 2; 6 sc in 2nd ch from hook. Work 2 sc in each sc around, then work even on 12 sc for 7 rnds. End off. Stuff legs; sew to front of body so egg will sit up.

HAT: With yellow, ch 2.

Rnd 1: 6 sc in 2nd ch from hook.

Rnd 2: 2 sc in each sc around.

Rnd 3: (2 sc in next sc, sc in next sc) 6 times.

Rnd 4: Sc in back lp of each sc around. Drop yellow.

Rnd 5: With blue, sc in each sc around. End off.

Rnds 6 and 7: With yellow, inc 4 sc in rnd—26 sc.

Rnd 8: Sc in each sc around. End off; leave end for sewing hat to head.

FINISHING: Sew 1″ loops of gold or brown yarn to forehead for hair. Sew hat in place over loops, stuffing hat first. Make black French knots for eyes. Embroider oval nose with rose floss in satin stitch. Embroider long smiling mouth with red floss in outline stitch. With pink floss, embroider lazy-daisy flower at each side of mouth. (See Stitch Details, page 105.)

Disk Doll

SIZE: 22″ tall.

MATERIALS: Knitting worsted, 12 ounces of assorted colors, including 3 ounces dark pink and 1 ounce dark red. Crochet hook size G. Tapestry needle. Polyester fiberfill.

GAUGE: 4 sts = 1″. (To test gauge, see page 108.)

DOLL: BODY: With dark pink, ch 20.

Rnd 1: Dc in 4th ch from hook, dc in each ch to last ch, 3 dc in last ch. Working on opposite side of starting ch, dc in each ch, dc in same ch with first dc—36 dc. Sl st in top of ch 3.

Rnd 2: Ch 3, dc in same ch with sl st, dc in each of next 17 dc, 3 dc in end dc, dc in each of next 17 dc, dc in same ch with first dc—40 dc. Sl st in top of ch 3.

Rnd 3: Ch 3, dc in next dc and in each dc around. Join. Repeat rnd 3 until piece is 6″ from start. Cut yarn, leaving long end for sewing. Sew first 6 sts each side of last st tog for shoulder. Leaving next 8 sts free each side for neck, sew last 6 sts each side tog for shoulder. Stuff body.

HEAD: With dark pink, ch 16. Sl st in first ch to form ring.

Rnd 1: Ch 1, sc in each ch around—16 sc. Join each rnd.

Rnd 2: Ch 1; working in back lp of each sc throughout head, work 2 sc in first sc, sc in 7 sc, 2 sc in next sc, sc in 7 sc—18 sc.

Rnd 3: Ch 1; 2 sc in first sc, sc in 7 sc, 2 sc in each of next 2 sc, sc in 7 sc, sc in last sc—22 sc.

Rnds 4-8: Continue to work in sc, inc 3 sts each side of head each rnd—52 sc.

Rnds 9 and 10: Work even.

Rnds 11-16: Dec 3 sts each side each rnd. End off.

Sew top edges tog. Stuff head. With white, embroider eyes in satin stitch; make brown pupils. Outline eyes and make lashes with black. Make 2 black sts for nose. Embroider mouth with red. (See Stitch Details, page 105.) For hair, thread double strand of dark red in tapestry needle. Stitching through head and leaving 1″ loops each stitch, make loops all over head. Sew head to neck, adding more stuffing before closing seam.

ARMS: With pink, ch 2.

Rnd 1: 6 sc in 2nd ch from hook.

Rnd 2: 2 sc in each sc around.

Rnd 3: (Sc in next sc, 2 sc in next sc) 6 times.

Rnds 4-6: Work even on 18 sc.

Rnd 7: (Sc in next 2 sc, sk next sc) 6 times. Stuff hand firmly.

Rnd 8: (Sc in next sc, sk next sc) 6 times. Sc in every other sc to close hole. Make a ch 8″ long. End off, leaving long end for sewing.

Disks (make 26 for each sleeve): With any color, ch 5. Sl st in first ch to form ring. Ch 3, work 16 dc in ring. Join; end off. Run in yarn ends.

SUIT (make 18 disks): With any color, ch 40. Sl st in first ch to form ring. Ch 2, hdc in each ch around. Join. Change color; ch 4 for first tr, * 2 tr in next st, tr in next st, repeat from * around, changing color as desired. Join; end off. Place 3 disks around neck; tack to body and shoulders as necessary to hold in place. Make a black ch 8″ long; form bow; tack to center front of top disk.

String 26 small disks for sleeves on each arm chain. Sew top of arm chains firmly to shoulders. Place remaining suit disks around

body. Tack in place at sides. Lowest one should be tacked all around.

LEGS: With double strand of black, work as for arms. Make ch 10″ long. End off, leaving long end for sewing.

Disks (make 30 for each leg): With any color, ch 5. Sl st in first ch to form ring. Ch 4, work 16 tr in ring. Join; end off. Run in yarn ends. String disks on leg chains. Sew top of leg chains to each side of body at lower edge.

Blondie and Butch

SIZE: 20″ tall.

MATERIALS: Rug yarn, 4-ounce skeins, 3 skeins red (A), 2 skeins each white (B) and eggshell (C), 1 skein each blue (D), yellow (E), black (F) and brown (G). Crochet hooks sizes H-8 and K-10½. Six packages 1″ "bone" rings. Two ⅞″ "bone" rings. Polyester or cotton stuffing. Four ⅝″ movable eyes. Two 1″ white buttons. Two ½″ black half-ball buttons. Scrap of black felt. Scissors.

GAUGE: 1 circle = 2½″ diameter (size K hook); 3 sc = 1″ (size H hook). (To test gauge, see page 108.)

CIRCLE PATTERN: With size K hook, work 12 sc in 1″ ring. Mark beg of each rnd.

Rnd 2: Work 2 sc in each sc.

Rnd 3: Sl st in each sc. End off.

BOY: HEAD: Beg at top, with size H hook and C, work 10 sc in ⅞″ ring. Mark beg of each rnd.

Rnd 1: Work 2 sc in each sc—20 sc.

Rnd 2: * Sc in next sc, 2 sc in next sc; repeat from *.

Rnd 3: * Sc in next 2 sc, 2 sc in next sc; repeat from *.

Rnd 4: * Sc in next 3 sc, 2 sc in next sc; repeat from *.

Rnds 5-11: Sc in each sc—50 sc.

Rnd 12: * Sc in next 3 sc, dec 1 st; repeat from *.

Rnds 13 and 14: Repeat rnd 5—40 sc.

Rnd 15: * Sc in next 2 sc, dec 1 st; repeat from *.

Rnds 16 and 17: Repeat rnd 5—30 sc.

Rnd 18: * Sc in next sc, dec 1 st; repeat from *.

Rnd 19: Repeat rnd 5—20 sc. Stuff.

Rnds 20 and 21: * Dec 1 st; repeat from *. End off, leaving a long tail for sewing.

BODY: With size H hook and A, ch 36; join with a sl st in first ch. Mark beg of each rnd.

Rnd 1: Sc in each st—36 sc. Work rnd 1, 13 times. With D, work rnd 1, 19 times. End off. Flatten piece. Sew tog along last D row. Stuff. Sew top edge tog. Sew head to body.

LEGS (make 2): Read directions for making a pompon below; with F, make a 3″ pompon, leaving a long tail for threading. Make 6 D, 3 C, 4 A, and 3 B circles, following the circle pattern. Thread tail of pompon through center of circles in following manner: A and B alternately, beg with A, 3 C and 6 D. Attach to bottom of body.

ARMS (make 2): Thread 5 C, then 6 A circles onto 2½″ C pompon. Attach to shoulder. Sew last circle to shoulder on top.

STRAPS (make 2): With D and size H hook, ch 34. Sc in 2nd ch from hook and in each ch across, ch 2, sc in each st on other side of foundation ch. End off. Sew one end to first D row on back. Crisscross strap and bring to front. Sew to first D row with button.

HAIR: With G, cut 3″ lengths of yarn for fringe. Beg in 14th rnd from bottom at back of head, insert hook under sc, fold 2 strands in half and pull through, then pull ends through lp. Continue in this manner, leaving face open, for 5 rnds towards top of head, then fill in remainder of rnds, forming bangs.

POMPON: Cut two cardboard disks desired size of pompon; cut ¼″ hole in center of both. Thread needle with two strands of yarn. Place disks together; cover with yarn, working through holes. Slip scissors between disks; cut all strands at outside edge. Draw strand of

yarn down between disks and wind several times very tightly around yarn; knot, leaving ends for attaching pompon. Remove cardboard disks and fluff out pompon.

FINISHING: Sew on eyes. Cut eyelashes from felt, using pattern, then glue under eyes. Sew on button for nose. With A, make couching st for mouth (see Stitch Details, page 105).

Eyelash

GIRL: Make head same as for boy.

With B, make body same as for boy. Make legs same as for boy, but alternate 4 A and 3 B circles, then 9 C. Make arms same as for boy, but thread 5 C, then 6 B circles.

HAIR: With E and size K hook, ch 50. Work 2 sc in each ch across. End off. Insert hook under top ring. Pull ends of curl through, forming lp, then pull ends through lp. Make 12 curls in same manner and attach to head. Line up curls around head and tack approximately 3½″ from top. Cut strands to measure 8″. Using 2 strands at once, form bangs by pulling through 2nd sc rnd.

SKIRT: With size H hook and A, ch 38; join with a sl st in first ch. Mark beg of each rnd.

Rnd 1: Sc in each st around.

Rnds 2 and 4: Dc in each st around.

Rnd 3: Dc in each dc, inc 8 sts evenly spaced.

Repeat rnds 3 and 4 two more times, join with a sl st.

Next Rnd: Working from left to right, with size K hook, * ch 1, sk 1 sc, sc in next sc; repeat from * around, join. End off.

BIB: Sc in front 9 sc of first rnd, ch 1 to turn all rows.

Rows 2-7: Sc in each sc. End off.

ARMBANDS: With D, work 7 sc along side of bib, ch 30.

Row 1: Dc in 2nd ch from hook and in each st of ch, then in 7 sc; ch 2, turn.

Row 2: Dc in each dc; ch 4, turn.

Rows 3 and 4: Dc in first dc, * ch 2, dc in next dc; repeat from *; ch 4 to turn. End off. Sew side edge of band to top edge of skirt, leaving last 2 rows of band free. Work other side the same. Put skirt on doll. Sew ends of bands tog at back, then tack bands to skirt, pulling bands to fit. Form remaining sections of bands in bow. Tack in place. Complete face same as for boy.

Marty Mouse

SIZE: 6″ plus tail.

MATERIALS: Knitting worsted, 1 ounce each of main color (MC) and contrasting color (CC). Crochet hook size J. Stuffing. Scraps of black felt. Glue.

GAUGE: 3 sc = 1″. (To test gauge, see page 108.)

MOUSE: BODY: Beg at nose, with MC, ch 4. Sl st in first ch to form ring.

Rnd 1: 2 sc in each ch around.

Rnds 2-7: Working in back lps only (throughout), * sc in 2 sts, 2 sc in next st, repeat from * for 6 rnds or until there are 50 sc in rnd.

Rnds 8-11: Work even on 50 sc for 4 rnds. Stuff.

Rnds 12-17: * Sc in 3 sts, sk next sc, repeat from * until there are 10 sc in rnd.

Rnd 18: Sl st in every other st until body opening is closed. End off.

TAIL: With CC, work 4 sc around end of mouse, work 15 rnds of 4 sc. End off. Close end of tail.

FEET: Join CC between rnds 8 and 9 on underside of body, work sc, hdc, 3 dc, hdc and sc all in the same st. End off. Tie two ends tog; tuck ends inside body. Repeat for other front foot on other side of the body. Work two back feet the same, making feet between rnds 13 and 14.

EARS: Join CC with sc in st on rnd 8, sc in each of next 8 sts, ch 1, turn. Working in back lps, * sc in next st, 2 sc in next st, repeat from * across. Turn. Working in free lps of original 8 sc, repeat from * to * across—24 sc.

Rnds 2 and 3: Sc in each sc around.

Rnds 4-6: Sl st in every other st until ear is closed. End off. Repeat ear on other side of head.

WHISKERS: Cut 4 pieces of CC 3″ long. Fold 2 strands in half, knot fringe through st on one side of nose. Repeat on other side of nose.

FINISHING: Tuck in all ends. Cut eyes and mouth from black felt; glue on.

Actual-size Patterns

Eye

Mouth

Pinafore Pattie

SIZE: 25″ tall.

MATERIALS: Worsted weight yarn, 4 ounces light green, 3 ounces pink, 2 ounces white, 1 ounce brown. Scrap of red. Crochet hook size F-5. Polyester fiberfill for stuffing. Two green shank-type buttons. Yarn needle. Long sewing needle. Thread.

DOLL: HEAD AND BODY: With pink, beg at top of head, ch 2.

Rnd 1: 6 sc in 2nd ch from hook.

Rnd 2: 2 sc in each sc around.

Rnd 3: (Sc in next sc, 2 sc in next sc) 6 times.

Rnd 4: Work even on 18 sc.

Rnd 5: (Sc in 2 sc, 2 sc in next sc) 6 times.

Rnd 6: (Sc in 2 sc, 2 sc in next sc) 8 times.

Rnd 7: Work even on 32 sc.

Rnd 8: (Sc in 3 sc, 2 sc in next sc) 8 times.

Rnds 9-17: Work even on 40 sc.

Rnd 18: (Sc in 8 sc, work 2 sc tog) 4 times.

Rnds 19 and 20: Work even on 36 sc.

Rnd 21: (Work 2 sc tog) 8 times, sc in each remaining sc.

Rnd 22: Work even on 28 sc.

Rnd 23: (Work 2 sc tog) 4 times, sc in each remaining sc.

Rnd 24: Work even on 24 sc. Work sc in next sc.

Rnd 25: Ch 1, turn; sc in 5 sc; ch 1, turn; sc in 13 sc, (work 2 sc tog) 4 times, sc in each of next 20 sts. End off. Fold head to find center back.

Body: Join white in center back st, sc in 5 sc, ch 4 (shoulder); sc in 2nd ch from hook and in next 2 ch, sc in 10 sc, ch 4 (shoulder); sc in 2nd ch from hook and in next 2 ch, sc in 5 sc. Mark end of rnd.

Rnd 2: Sc in 5 sc, 3 sc in each ch, 3 sc on shoulder, sc in 10 sc, 3 sc in each ch, 3 sc on shoulder, sc in 5 sc—32 sc.

Rnd 3: Sc around, inc 1 st at end of each shoulder.

Rnd 4: Work even—34 sc.

Rnd 5: Sc around, inc 1 st at each shoulder and 2 at front center, evenly spaced.

Rnd 6: Work even—38 sc.

Rnd 7: Inc 1 st at back and front center.

Rnds 8 and 9: Work even on 40 sc.

Rnd 10: Inc 2 sts in back and 2 sts in front.

Rnds 11 and 12: Work even on 44 sc.

Rnd 13: Repeat rnd 10.

Rnds 14-26: Work even on 48 sc. Cut white.

Rnds 27-29: With green, work even on 48 sc.

Rnd 30: (Sc in 6 sc, work 2 sc tog) 6 times.

Rnd 31: Work even on 42 sc.

Rnd 32: (Sc in 5 sc, work 2 sc tog) 6 times.

Rnds 33-36: Work even on 36 sc. End off. Stuff.

BOTTOM: Beg at back edge, with green, ch 11.

Row 1: Sc in 2nd ch from hook and in each ch. Ch 1, turn each row.

Row 2: Working in sc, inc 1 sc each side.

Row 3: Work even—12 sc.

Rows 4-7: Repeat rows 2 and 3 twice—16 sc.

Row 8: Dec 1 sc each side.

Row 9: Work even.

Rows 10-12: Repeat rows 8, 9, 8. End off. Sew bottom to doll.

LEGS:

Thigh: With pink, ch 20. Sl st in first ch to form ring.

Rnds 1-8: Work even on 20 sc.

Rnd 9: (Sc in 8 sc, work 2 sc tog) twice.

Rnds 10-17: Work even on 18 sc.

Rnd 18: Dec 1 sc in rnd.

Rnds 19-22: Work even on 17 sc. End off.

Lower Leg: With pink, ch 16. Sl st in first ch to form ring.

Rnds 1-14: Work even on 16 sc. Cut pink.

Rnds 15-20: With white, work even.

Rnd 21: Dec 1 sc, work to end.

Rnd 22: Ch 5, sc in 2nd ch from hook and in next 3 ch, sc in 15 sc around.

Rnd 23: Sc in 4 ch, 2 sc in next sc, sc in each sc around. Cut white.

Rnd 24: With brown, work around, inc 1 sc at front of foot.

Rnds 25-28: Work even.

Rnd 29: Dec 1 sc at toe and 1 sc at heel. End off. Sew legs flat across; stuff before sewing last seam. Sew thigh to lower leg. Sew up slit at bottom of shoe.

Shoe Strap (make 2): With brown, ch 11. Work 1 row of 10 sc. Sew on.

Button: With white, ch 2; 2 sc in 2nd ch from hook; sew into a ball; sew to shoe.

Cuff of Sock: With white, ch 21. Work 1 row of 20 sc. Sew on.

Knee: With pink, ch 2.

Rnd 1: 5 sc in 2nd ch from hook.

Rnd 2: Work 2 sc in each sc around. End off. Stuff with yarn end; sew, wrong side out, over knee joint.

Panty Legs: With green, ch 22. Sl st in first ch to form ring. Work 3 rnds even on 22 sc. Slip over leg and sew to panties.

ARMS:

Upper Arm: With white, ch 16. Sl st in first ch to form ring. Work 12 rnds even on 16 sc. Cut white.

Rnds 13-18: With pink, work even.

Rnd 19: Dec 1 sc. End off. Stuff and sew top of arm flat across. Sew elbow end flat across in the opposite direction.

Lower Arm: With pink, ch 15. Sl st in first ch to form ring.

Rnds 1-4: Work even on 15 sc.

Rnd 5: Dec 1 sc in rnd.

Rnds 6-12: Work even on 14 sc.

Rnds 13 and 14: Dec 1 sc in each rnd.

Rnd 15: Work even on 12 sc.

Rnd 16: (2 sc in next sc, sc in 2 sc) 4 times.

Rnd 17: Work even on 16 sc.

Rnd 18: (Sc in 7 sc, 2 sc in next sc) twice.

Rnds 19 and 20: Work even on 18 sc.

Rnd 21: (Work 2 tog, sc in 7 sc) twice.

Rnd 22: (Work 2 tog) 8 times.

Rnd 23: Work even. End off. Run yarn through sts. Stuff arm. Place arm on flat surface so hand is flat. Sew arm flat across at elbow. Sew to upper arm. Make trim for sleeve as for sock cuff. Make elbow same as knee. Sew arms to shoulders.

PINAFORE:

Bib: With green, ch 12.

Row 1: Sc in 2nd ch from hook and in each ch across. Ch 3, turn.

Row 2: Dc in 2nd st and in each sc across. Ch 1, turn.

Row 3: Sc in each st across. Ch 3, turn.

Rows 4-9: Repeat rows 2 and 3. End off.

Skirt: With green, ch 50. Sc in 2nd ch from hook and in each ch across. Ch 1, turn each sc row.

Rows 2 and 3: Work even in sc. At end of row 3, ch 2, turn.

Row 4: Dc across. Ch 1, turn.

Row 5: Sc across, inc 1 sc in every 4th st. Ch 2, turn.

Row 6: Work even in dc. Ch 1, turn.

Rows 7 and 8: Repeat rows 5 and 6.

Rows 9-12: Work even, alternating sc and dc rows.

Row 13: Sc across, inc 12 sts evenly spaced across.

Row 14: Work even in dc.

Row 15: Work even in sc. End off.

RUFFLE (make 2): With green, ch 25.

Row 1: 2 sc in 2nd ch from hook and in each ch to end. Ch 2, turn.

Row 2: 2 dc in each sc. Ch 1, turn.

Row 3: Sc in each dc across.

STRAP (make 2): With green, ch 5. Work in rows of 4 sc until strap is long enough to go from top of bib to back of skirt.

FINISHING: Sew bib to skirt; sew back skirt seam; sew on straps; sew ruffles to straps.

Hair is made by winding yarn around pencil. Place end of yarn up pencil ½", then start winding over pencil. Cut yarn, leaving 8". Thread needle with end, run needle through yarn, up pencil. Slide windings off pencil, pull up a bit, adjust curl, sew to head. For top curls, pull up more. Tie bow in hair.

Press face in a bit, about half way down; sew on button eyes. Make pink nose like shoe button, or embroider dots for nose. Embroider mouth with red, lashes with brown.

PART IV

GENERAL DIRECTIONS

Enlarging the Pattern

If the pattern is given on squares, you must enlarge it to its actual size by drawing a grid on a sheet of paper with the same number of squares as in the grid of the pattern, but making each square of your grid the size directed (usually 1″). The grid can be easily drawn on graph paper. Or, if graph paper is not available, on plain paper mark dots around the edges 1″ apart (or the size directed) and form a grid by joining the dots across opposite sides of the paper. Then copy the design onto your grid, square by square. Glue to cardboard and cut on lines of design, ignoring the grid lines. An easier procedure is to have the design enlarged by photostat, if such a service is available in your area.

Appliqué

Choose a fabric that is closely woven and firm enough so a clean edge results when the pieces are cut. Press fabric smooth. There are two methods of transferring appliqué patterns to fabric:

TO TRANSFER LARGE DESIGNS: Mark a pattern on paper for each appliqué piece; do not cut out. Place paper on right side of fabric, inserting dressmaker's tracing (carbon) paper between fabric and pattern. Go over lines of pattern with tracing wheel or a dry ball-point pen, to transfer design. Remove pattern and carbon. Mark a second outline ¼″ outside design outline. Appliqué as directed below.

TO TRANSFER SMALL DESIGNS: For each motif, make a cardboard pattern: Trace design; do not cut out. Glue tracing paper to thin, stiff cardboard and let dry; cut along traced line. Place cardboard pattern on right side of fabric. Holding sharp, hard pencil at an outward angle (light-colored pencil on dark fabric and dark pencil on light fabric), mark around pattern. When marking several pieces on the same fabric, leave at least ½″ between pieces. Mark a second outline ¼″ outside design outline. Appliqué as directed below.

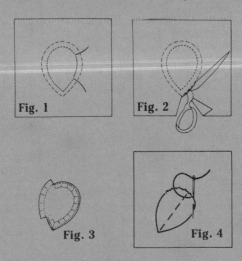

Fig. 1 Fig. 2 Fig. 3 Fig. 4

TO APPLIQUÉ BY HAND: Using matching thread and small stitches, machine-stitch all around design outline, as shown in **Fig. 1.** This makes edge easier to turn and neater in appearance. Cut out appliqué on the outside line, as in **Fig. 2.** For a smooth edge, clip into seam allowance at curved edges and corners, then turn seam allowance to back, just inside stitching as shown in **Fig. 3,** and press. (**Note:** You may prefer to place some pieces so they overlap the extended seam allowance of adjacent pieces; study overall design before turning under all seam allowances.) Pin and baste the appliqués on the background, the underneath pieces first, and slip-stitch in place with tiny stitches. See **Fig. 4.**

TO APPLIQUÉ BY MACHINE: Cut out appliqués on outside lines. Pin and baste appliqués in place; do not turn under excess fabric. Straight-stitch around appliqués on marked lines. Trim away excess fabric to ⅛" from straight stitching. Set sewing machine for close zigzag stitch as directed (¼" wide or less). Zigzag around appliqués, covering straight stitching and excess fabric.

Embroidery

TO PREPARE FABRIC: To prevent fabric from raveling, bind all raw edges with masking tape, whipstitch edges by hand, or machine-stitch ⅛" in from all edges.

FRAMES/HOOPS: Work embroidery in a frame or hoop. With the material held tautly and evenly, your stitches are more likely to be neat and accurate than if the fabric were held in hand while working.

TO BEGIN AND END A STRAND: Cut floss or yarn into 18" strands. To begin a strand, leave an end on back and work over it to secure; to end, run needle under four or five stitches on back or take a few tiny backstitches. Do not make knots. Fasten off the thread when ending each motif, rather than carrying it to another motif.

TO REMOVE EMBROIDERY: When a mistake has been made, run a needle, eye first, under the stitches. Pull the embroidery away from the fabric; cut carefully with small scissors pressed hard against the needle. Pick out the cut portion of the embroidery and catch loose ends of the remaining stitches on back by pulling the ends under the stitches with a crochet hook.

FOR COUNTED CROSS-STITCH: For counted cross-stitch on even-weave fabrics, work stitches over a counted number of threads both horizontally and vertically, following a chart. Each symbol on the chart represents one stitch. Different symbols represent different colors.

For fabrics such as Aida cloth or hardanger, follow the mesh of the coarse flat weave (much like needlepoint canvas), where holes are obvious. Each "thread" is actually made up of four or more fine threads in a group and stitches are worked from hole to hole.

For counted cross-stitch on gingham fabric, work stitches over checks, so that one complete cross-stitch covers one check.

When working cross-stitches, work underneath stitches in one direction and top stitches in the opposite direction, making sure all strands lie smooth and flat; allow needle to hang freely from work occasionally, to untwist floss. Make crosses touch by inserting needle in same hole used for adjacent stitch (see Stitch Details).

TO FINISH: When your embroidered piece is completed, finish off the back neatly by running ends into the back of the work and clipping off any excess threads. Place piece face down on a well padded surface and press, using a steam iron, or regular iron and damp pressing cloth. Press lightly from the center outward. For embroidery that is raised from the surface of the background, use extra thick, soft padding, such as a thick blanket.

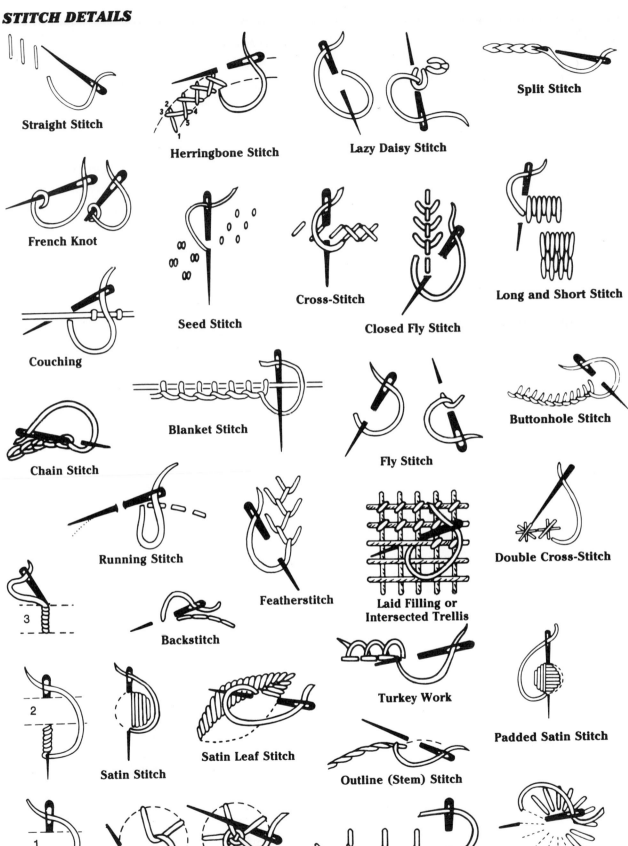

Straight Stitch

Herringbone Stitch

Lazy Daisy Stitch

Split Stitch

French Knot

Seed Stitch

Cross-Stitch

Closed Fly Stitch

Long and Short Stitch

Couching

Chain Stitch

Blanket Stitch

Fly Stitch

Buttonhole Stitch

Running Stitch

Featherstitch

Laid Filling or Intersected Trellis

Double Cross-Stitch

Backstitch

Turkey Work

Satin Stitch

Satin Leaf Stitch

Outline (Stem) Stitch

Padded Satin Stitch

Bullion Stitch

Woven Spider Web Stitch

Cretan or Open Cretan Stitch

Radiating Straight Stitch

Crochet

CHAIN STITCH: To make first loop on hook, grasp yarn about 2″ from end between left thumb and index finger. With right hand, lap long strand over short end, forming a loop. Hold loop in place with left thumb and index finger. Grasp hook in right hand, insert hook through loop, catch strand with hook and draw it through loop. Pull end and long strand in opposite directions to close loop around hook.

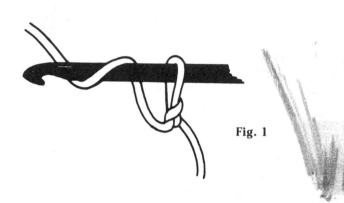

Fig. 1

Figure 1: To make your first chain stitch, pass hook under yarn on index finger and catch strand with hook.

Draw yarn through loop on hook. This makes one chain stitch. Repeat last step until you have as many chains as you need. One loop always remains on hook. Practice making all chains uniform.

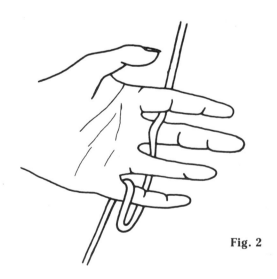

Fig. 2

Figure 2: Weave yarn through left hand.

SINGLE CROCHET:

Fig. 1

Figure 1: Insert hook in second chain from hook. Yarn over hook.

Fig. 2

Figure 2: Draw yarn through chain. Two loops on hook.

Fig. 3

Figure 3: Yarn over hook. Draw yarn through 2 loops on hook. One single crochet has been made.

Fig. 4

Figure 4: Work a single crochet in each chain stitch. At end of row, chain 1 and turn work around.

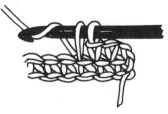

Fig. 5

Figure 5: Insert hook under both top loops of first stitch, yarn over hook and draw through stitch. Yarn over and through 2 loops on hook. Work a single crochet in same way in each stitch across row.

Fig. 6

Figure 6: To make a ridge stitch or slipper stitch, work rows of single crochet by inserting hook in back loop only of each single crochet.

HOW TO INCREASE 1 SINGLE CROCHET: Work 2 stitches in 1 stitch.

HOW TO DECREASE 1 SINGLE CROCHET: Pull up a loop in 1 stitch, pull up a loop in next stitch (3 loops on hook), yarn over hook, draw through all 3 loops at once.

SLIP STITCH: Insert hook in work. Yarn over hook and draw through both the stitch and the loop on hook. Slip stitch makes a firm finishing edge. A single slip stitch is used for joining a chain to form a ring.

HALF DOUBLE CROCHET:

Fig. 1

Figure 1: Yarn over hook. Insert hook in 3rd chain from hook.

Fig. 2

Figure 2: Yarn over hook, draw through chain. Yarn over hook again.

Fig. 3

Figure 3: Draw through all 3 loops on hook. One half double crochet has been made.

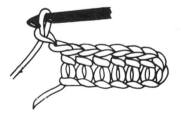

Fig. 4

Figure 4: Work a half double crochet in each chain across. At end of row, ch 2 and turn work.

DOUBLE CROCHET:

Fig. 1

Figure 1: Yarn over hook. Insert hook in 4th chain from hook.

Fig. 2

Figure 2: Yarn over hook. Draw through chain. There are 3 loops on hook.

Fig. 3

Figure 3: Yarn over hook. Draw through 2 loops on hook. There are 2 loops on hook. Yarn over hook.

Fig. 4

Figure 4: Draw yarn through remaining 2 loops on hook. One double crochet has been made. When you have worked a double crochet in each chain across, chain 3 and turn work. In most directions, the turning chain 3 counts as first double crochet of next row. In working the 2nd row, skip the first stitch and work a double crochet in the 2 top loops of each double crochet across. The last double crochet of each row is worked in the top chain of the chain 3 turning chain.

Treble or Triple Crochet (tr): With 1 loop on hook put yarn over hook twice, insert in 5th chain from hook, pull loop through. Yarn over and draw through 2 loops at a time 3 times. At end of a row, chain 4 and turn. Chain 4 counts as first treble of next row.

HOW TO TURN YOUR WORK: In crochet a certain number of ch sts are needed at the end of each row to bring work into position for the next row. Then work is turned so reverse side is facing the crocheter. Follow the stitch table below for the number of ch sts to make a turn.

Single crochet (sc)	Ch 1 to turn
Half double crochet (half dc or hdc)	Ch 2 to turn
Double crochet (dc)	Ch 3 to turn
Treble crochet (tr)	Ch 4 to turn
Double treble crochet (dtr)	Ch 5 to turn
Treble treble crochet (tr tr)	Ch 6 to turn

CROCHET ABBREVIATIONS

ch—chain stitch	sc—single crochet
st—stitch	sl st—slip stitch
sts—stitches	dc—double crochet
lp—loop	hdc—half double crochet
inc—increase	tr—treble or triple crochet
dec—decrease	dtr—double treble crochet
rnd—round	tr tr—treble treble crochet
beg—beginning	bl—block
sk—skip	sp—space
p—picot	pat—pattern
tog—together	yo—yarn over hook

MEASURING YOUR GAUGE: Most knitting and crochet directions include a stitch gauge. The stitch gauge gives the number of stitches to the inch with the yarn and hook or needles recommended in the pattern stitch. The directions are based on the given gauge. The gauge (or tension) at which you work controls of the size of each finished piece. It is therefore essential to work to the gauge given for each item if you want it to be the correct size. To test your gauge, cast on 20–30 stitches, using the hook or needles specified. Work in the pattern stitches for 3″. Smooth out your swatch and pin it down. Measure across 2″ and place pins 2″ apart. Count number of stitches between pins. If you have more stitches to the inch than directions

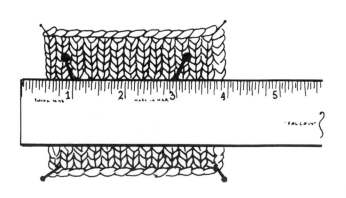

specify, you are working too tightly; use a larger hook or needles. If you have fewer stitches to the inch, you are working too loosely; use a smaller hook or needles.

Most patterns give a row gauge, too. Although the proper length does not usually depend on the row gauge (directions usually give lengths in inches rather than rows), in some patterns it is important to have the proper row gauge, too.

HOW TO FOLLOW DIRECTIONS: An asterisk (*) is often used in crochet directions to indicate repetition. For example, when directions read "* 2 dc in next st, 1 dc in next st, repeat from * 4 times" this means to work directions after first * until second * is reached, then go back to first * 4 times more. Work 5 times in all.

When parentheses ( ) are used to show repetition, work directions within parentheses as many times as specified. For example, "(dc, ch 1) 3 times" means to do what is within ( ) 3 times altogether.

"Work even" in directions means to work in same stitch without increasing or decreasing.

Knitting

CASTING ON: There are many ways of casting on stitches. The method shown here is only one of them. It gives you a strong and elastic edge.

Fig. 1

Figure 1: Allow enough yarn for the number of stitches to be cast on (about ½″ per stitch for lighter weight yarns such as baby yarns, 1″ per stitch for heavier yarns such as knitting worsted, more for bulky yarns on large needles). Make a slip loop on needle and tighten knot gently.

Fig. 2

Figure 2: Hold needle in right hand with short end of yarn over left thumb. Weave strand that comes from ball through right hand, over index finger, under second, over third, and under fourth finger.

Fig. 3

Figure 3: Bring needle forward to make a loop over left thumb. Insert needle from left to right in loop; bring yarn in right hand under, then over point of needle, and draw yarn through loop with tip of needle.

Fig. 4

Figure 4: Keeping right hand in same position, tighten stitch on needle gently with left hand. You now have 2 stitches on needle. Repeat Figures 3 and 4 for required number of stitches.

KNIT STITCH:

Fig. 5

Figure 5: Hold needle with cast on stitches in left hand and yarn in same position as for casting on in right hand. Insert point of needle from left to right in first stitch.

Fig. 6

Figure 6: Bring yarn under and over point of right needle.

Fig. 7

Figure 7: Draw yarn through stitch with point of needle.

Fig. 8

Figure 8: Allow loop on left needle to slip off needle. Loop on right needle is your first knit stitch. Repeat from Figure 5 in each loop across row. When you have finished knitting one row, place needle with stitches in left hand ready to start next row.

GARTER STITCH: If you work row after row of knit stitch, you are working garter stitch.

PURL STITCH:

Fig. 9

Figure 9: To purl, insert needle from right to left in stitch on left needle. Bring yarn over

and under point of right needle. Draw yarn back through stitch and allow loop on left needle to slip off needle.

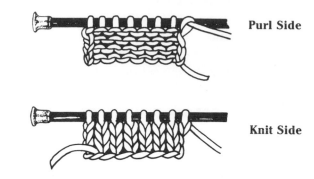

Purl Side

Knit Side

Stockinette Stitch: If you work one row of knit stitch and one row of purl stitch alternately, you are working stockinette stitch.

Reverse Stockinette Stitch: If you work one row of purl stitch and one row of knit stitch alternately, you are working reverse stockinette stitch.

BINDING OFF:

Fig. 10

Figure 10: Knit the first two stitches. Insert left needle from left to right through front of first stitch. Lift first stitch over second stitch and over tip of right needle. One stitch has been bound off, one stitch remains on right needle. Knit another stitch. Again lift first stitch over second stitch and off right needle. Continue across until all stitches have been bound off. One loop remains on needle. Cut yarn, pull end through loop and tighten knot.

TO INCREASE ONE STITCH: There are several ways to increase a stitch.

Method 1 is illustrated. Knit 1 stitch in the usual way but do not slip it off left needle. Bring right needle behind left needle, insert it

from right to left in same stitch (called "the back of the stitch") and make another knit stitch. Slip stitch off left needle. To increase 1 stitch on the purl stitch, purl 1 stitch but do not slip it off left needle. Bring yarn between needles to back, knit 1 stitch in back of same stitch.

Method 2: Pick up horizontal strand between stitch just knitted and next stitch, place it on left needle. Knit 1 stitch in back of this strand, thus twisting it.

Method 3: Place right needle behind left needle. Insert right needle in stitch below next stitch, knit this stitch, then knit stitch above it in the usual way.

TO DECREASE ONE STITCH: On the right side of work, knit 2 stitches together as in illustration, through the front of the stitches (the decrease slants to the right), or through the back of the stitches (the decrease slants to the left). On the purl side, purl 2 stitches together. Another decrease stitch is called "psso" (pass slip stitch over). When directions say "sl 1, k 1, psso," slip first stitch (take it from left to right needle without knitting it), knit next stitch, then bring slip stitch over knit stitch as in binding off.

KNITTING ABBREVIATIONS

k—knit	psso—pass slip stitch over
p—purl	inc—increase
st—stitch	dec—decrease
sts—stitches	beg—beginning
yo—yarn over	pat—pattern
sl—slip	lp—loop
sk—skip	MC—main color
tog—together	CC—contrasting color
rnd—round	dp—double-pointed

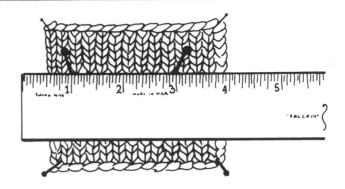

MEASURING YOUR GAUGE: Most knitting and crochet directions include a stitch gauge. The stitch gauge gives the number of stitches to the inch with the yarn and hook or needles recommended in the pattern stitch. The directions are based on the given gauge. The gauge (or tension) at which you work controls the size of each finished piece. It is therefore essential to work to the gauge given for each item if you want it to be the correct size. To test your gauge, cast on 20–30 stitches, using the hook or needles specified. Work in the pattern stitches for 3″. Smooth out your swatch and pin it down. Measure across 2″ and place pins 2″ apart. Count number of stitches between pins. If you have more stitches to the inch than directions specify, you are working too tightly; use a larger hook or needles. If you have fewer stitches to the inch, you are working too loosely; use a smaller hook or needles.

Most patterns give a row gauge, too. Although the proper length does not usually depend on the row gauge (directions usually give lengths in inches rather than rows), in some patterns it is important to have the proper row gauge, too.

HOW TO FOLLOW DIRECTIONS: When parentheses ( ) are used to show repetition, work directions within parentheses as many times as specified. For example, "(K 3, p 2) 5 times" means to do all that is specified in parentheses 5 times in all.

"Place a marker on needle" in directions means to place a safety pin, paperclip, or bought plastic stitch marker on the needle between the stitches. It is slipped from one needle to the other to serve as a mark on following rows.

SHEEP

ANGEL

SHEPHERD

CROWNS

GIFTS

MANGER END

HALO

BABE

STAR

JOSEPH

HALO

WISE MAN

MARY

BASES
A   B   C